MORE THAN PEANUTS

MORE THAN PEANUTS

The Unlikely Partnership
of Tom Huston and
George Washington Carver

EDITH POWELL

FOREWORD BY WALTER A. HILL
READER'S NOTE BY BERT HITCHCOCK

NEWSOUTH BOOKS
an imprint of
The University of Georgia Press
Athens

NSB

Published by NewSouth Books,
an imprint of the University of Georgia Press
Athens, Georgia 30602
www.ugapress.org/imprints/newsouth-books/

Designed by Randall Williams
Printed and bound by Books International

The paper in this book meets the guidelines for
permanence and durability of the Committee on
Production Guidelines for Book Longevity of the
Council on Library Resources.

Most NewSouth/University of Georgia Press titles are
available from popular e-book vendors.

Printed in the United States of America
22 23 24 25 26 P 5 4 3 2 1

PUBLISHER'S CATALOGING-IN-PUBLICATION DATA
Names: Powell, Edith, 1940– , author.
Title: More than peanuts : the unlikely partnership of Tom Huston and George
Washington Carver / Edith Powell; contribution by Bert Hitchcock; foreword by
Walter A. Hill; afterword by Marceline Egnin.
Description: Montgomery : NewSouth Books, [2022]
Identifiers: LCCN 2022941743 | ISBN 9781588384461 (paperback) |
ISBN 9781588384591 (ebook)
Subjects: LCSH. Alabama—History—1819–1950. | Alabama—Biography. |
Alabama—History. | Business enterprises—Southern States. | Industries—Southern
States. | Peanut industry. | Peanut products. | Plant diseases. | Plant diseases—
Research. | Southern States—Race relations—History. | Southern States—Race
relations—History—20th century. | Southern States—History. | Southern
States—History—1865–1951.

*The Black Belt, defined by its dark, rich soil, stretches across central Alabama. It
was the heart of the cotton belt. It was and is a place of great beauty, of extreme
wealth and grinding poverty, of pain and joy. Here we take our stand, listening
to the past, looking to the future.*

In memory of Dr. Allan Edgar, Poultry Science Department, Auburn University, for accepting me into the Genetics PhD Program because he believed that I was smart enough,

and

In honor of Dean Walter Hill, College of Agriculture and Environmental Sciences, Tuskegee University, for making a place for me in his eminent research program because he believed that I could make a contribution.

Born in a then remote Alabama County and reared in an equally rural Texas area, he [Tom] had few educational advantages and no opportunities to help him on his way. But, his intense motivation propelled him to his triumphants. Hard work, total dedication, imagination, inventiveness brought the five cent peanut bag into being and turned the lowly Spanish peanut into little gold nuggets.

—AUTHOR UNKNOWN

At work, Carver was "the connector all by himself." He was the person in the lab doing the basic research thinking, the applied research thinking, tying it to the land, trying to tie it to business, and he had very few people around him to interact with him as he did this.

—DR. WALTER HILL,
TUSKEGEE UNIVERSITY

Contents

Foreword

WALTER A. HILL

First, as an African American, I understand the disgust, fear and horror George Washington Carver felt when he witnessed the lynching in Olathe, Kansas. Also, we will never know the impacts on Carver of being stolen by 'slave catchers' and then separated from his mother as a child. Every interaction with white people had to be carefully weighed by Carver on his life's journey. W. E. B. Dubois describes such as "a peculiar sensation. This double-consciousness, this sense of always looking at one's self through the eyes of others, of measuring one's soul by the tape of a world that looks on in amused contempt and pity. One ever feels his two-ness—an American, a negro . . ." The events in his life led Carver to accept the invitation to leave Iowa State College (all white people) and go to Tuskegee (all Black people).

Having worked at Tuskegee University for forty-four years, including as Dean of Agriculture, Experiment Station Research Director, and Extension Administrator, I gained an insider view and learned a lot about George Washington Carver's time at Tuskegee. Thanks to Edith Powell's book, I have learned more. Carver had challenges at Tuskegee. And Carver's multiple, God-given, and work-honed gifts and perspectives demanded outlets for expression to a global audience. As Carver wrote to Bob Barry ". . .there is always a something that encourages me to push ahead." Tuskegee is rural, local and global; it simultaneously draws in and reaches out to the world and beyond. Thus, we are not surprised that Huston sought out Carver to help him solve the problem of 'how to put salt on the inside of peanuts instead of putting oil and salt on the outside.' And that Barry and Grady Porter of the Huston Company teamed-up with Carver to identify and control peanut diseases in order to optimize crop yields, across the southern states.

The challenges associated with peanuts were many during 1928–32. The team was actively engaged in learning and problem-solving. They shared findings from ongoing experiments and observations at farms, research plots and laboratories. Through their passion to find answers, they encouraged each other. Such work intensity, driven by a common goal, brings people together. Carver was needed as a team member. His experience, power of observation, and scientific skills made the difference in the day-to-day outcomes and long term impacts of the team. However, Edith reminds us that the time was one of deep segregation; lines were sharply drawn based on race.

Carver was open and accepting to interactions from the Tom Huston Company, but it was the steadfast communications from Barry that convinced Carver of the Huston Company's sincerity toward his humanity. Barry made sure to compliment Carver for his contributions and give him credit for his accomplishments, including co-authoring publications or publishing thousands of copies of Carver's seminal work on Peanut Diseases. Their letters sounded like friends and colleagues sharing information.

At Tuskegee University I worked with people of all races, from many countries. Two white people, Phil Loretan and Ron Shumack, came to mind, as the relationship between Carver and Barry was unveiled in Edith's book. With Phil it was the National Aeronautics and Space Administration (NASA) project that sent plant experiments from Tuskegee University into space, and with Ron it was the Alabama Agricultural Land Grant Alliance that initiated shared research and funding among Alabama A&M, Auburn and Tuskegee universities. In both cases, as a result of respecting and valuing all team members, barriers were broken, work and communications were optimum, and measurable impacts resulted that contributed to the larger society.

Through her book, Edith documents and shares the unlikely partnership of Tom Huston and George Washington Carver that benefited farmers, Experiment Station Researchers, Extension Agents, related businesses, and consumers. The Huston Company profited and its employees Bob Barry and Grady Porter learned a lot about peanut diseases, nutrition and physiology. What did Carver gain? Respect for and acceptance of his expertise (genius) mattered to him. He valued being a member of a team that manifested integrative research-extension. The connection to the broader community was important, as expressed in his words "The Tom Huston Peanut company's plan interests me more than anything that I have come in contact with, as it is of real service to the people in general and to Southern Agriculture in particular." Important to him, and appreciated by the black world and beyond, was that his work, innovations and contributions came from a historically black university. What did Carver not get? Increased funding and resources to support his significant work. Such funding went to others . . .

Walter Hill joined the faculty at Tuskegee Institute (now Tuskegee University) in 1977 and served as dean of agriculture 1987–2022.

Preface

This story is told, for the most part, through letters written by George Washington Carver and to Carver by his colleagues. The letters are located in the George Washington Carver Collection in the Tuskegee University Archives. Purposefully, no effort was made to source other archival collections. Additionally, there is no intent to be all inclusive of every possible letter or article relating to this story. The author is certain that others exist elsewhere, but it is the intent of the author to highlight the holdings of the Tuskegee University Archives. While there are more than three hundred Hollinger boxes of letters, documents, articles, and clippings in the George Washington Carver collection at Tuskegee, the inclusions in this text are from 1924 through 1934 and have been carefully chosen from the approximately seven hundred letters related to the Carver-Huston story.

It was of critical importance to the author that the essence of the letters not be altered in any way. In letters and documents quoted in the text, the wording has been preserved much as written, including typos and misspellings; I trust the readers' discernment to recognize where these appear. Each letter was selected because of its contribution to and impact on the story details. Only relevant excerpts have been reproduced from some letters, but the texts of the letters have not been otherwise altered. Brackets [ ] indicate where the author inserted a word or words for clarification, asterisks * indicate additional notes or references, and ellipses . . . indicate omissions of unrelated content.

The Appendix contains some of the attachments to the selected letters because they demonstrate the level, scope, time, and complexity of the work that was done by both Carver and the Tom Huston team.

In addition, three boxes of letters, patents, photographs, and paintings of Tom Huston are located in the Columbus State University Archives in

Columbus, Georgia. The Archives also hold a vertical file containing two folders, one labeled "Tom Huston-Bio/Personal," and the other labeled "Tom Huston Company." All documents and articles used are paraphrased to represent the sources as truly as possible.

Mr. Huston was a shy man and made very few personal appearances. There is a paucity of information available. Efforts are ongoing to identify additional documents related to Tom Huston. Sadly, according to information obtained at the office of the current owner, the Tom's Foods Archives are no longer available. The author attempted to obtain any educational documents designed and used in the little museum established by the team during the time of the public relations blitz.

ACKNOWLEDGMENTS

When one reaches this section of writing a book, there comes the realization of how many people need to be thanked for helping to make the completion of the manuscript possible. Without them, there would be no manuscript.

All who know me know that I am computer illiterate. I know what is supposed to happen, but when it doesn't—due to something only I can do—I panic. And, I do mean, panic. Therefore, I must first thank my daughters, Elizabeth Gregory North and Rebecca Gregory Ross, and my grandson, Gregory Veal, for constantly rushing to my aid when I mistakenly pushed the wrong button and could not find my document the next minute. Gregory's long-suffering patience in teaching me to scan, get the scan to the desktop and into a file that I could locate again cannot be understated, nor undervalued. For the three years that I have been working on this manuscript, they have willingly dropped whatever they were doing and come to my aid to provide needed support and assistance.

To my sister, Betty Powell Fisher, and my BFF, Elaine W. Helms, my heartfelt thanks for the early reading of the manuscript and offering of needed editorial feedback. Also, additional thanks to sister, Bet, for her willingness to drive me to the Columbus State University archives and assist me in searching the file for more information on Tom Huston. And, to Elaine, for making possible the trips to the peanut fields in the Daphne, Alabama, area to allow me to jump out and go into the fields to photograph during different steps of the growing and harvesting process.

To my good friend and colleague, Dana R. Chandler, Archivist, Tuskegee University, my forever gratitude for your support since the beginning of this journey. I thank you for making it possible to spend hours of pure pleasure reading through the hundreds of letters of correspondence to and from Carver in the George Washington Carver Collection, and, for permission to use correspondence and photographs in the manuscript. My thanks also to Cheryl Ferguson, Assistant Archivist, for her invaluable assistance. Having been privileged to work with her for several years, I am grateful that she is always willing to answer my questions and to help in locating needed documents. And to Lonice Potts Middleton, a longtime colleague, fellow researcher, and guru of the photographs in the Tuskegee University archives, I owe thanks for always being on the lookout for photographs of Carver that might be appropriate for inclusion in this manuscript. Thanks also to Ryan Campbell of the TU Archives for assistance in transferring copies of photographs.

The staff at the Columbus State University Archives Archivist, David Owings and Archival Associate Jessie Merrell were extraordinarily supportive from the very beginning of this journey. During my several trips there I also received assistance from Tom Converse, and Martha Ragan, Archival Assistants, and volunteers. Their help was invaluable in pointing out the most important boxes that would contain the information I was searching for. I am also grateful to the Archives for granting permission to use the Tom Huston materials from the Tom Huston Collection (MC 37). My thanks also must go to John Varner, Special Collections and Archives, Auburn University Libraries for his assistance in locating the correct number of Alabama Bulletin No 180. To Susan Floyd, Texas State Library and Archives Comission, much appreciation for permission to use the article by Rebecca Romanchuk.

To my colleague, Dr. Bert Hitchcock, retired Emeritus Professor, Auburn University, I expressed my extreme inability to transfer "feelings" from my heart to paper. I am in awe of those, like Bert, who possess the skills to be able to write so that the reader literally loses him/herself within the story.

Bert was gracious to read the draft manuscript and give me feedback as to whether it was a good enough story to even approach a potential publisher. He not only felt that the story needed to be published, but he suggested the title and also agreed to write a Reader's Note. I remember breathing a huge sigh of relief when he shared his thoughts. He continues to provide support and answers to my questions. For my previous publications, I have had co-authors. This is the first time I have been the sole author. Many times, along this journey, I have come to realize that having someone to provide honest, respectful criticism is paramount to an author's energy to continue the effort. I am thankful for his kindness and mentorship.

For many years Dr. Walter Hill, Dean, College of Agriculture and Environmental Sciences at Tuskegee University, has been a mentor and friend. Dr. Hill is the long-time keeper and protector of the legacy of Carver, and he frequently lectures on the history of that legacy. It was natural, therefore, for me to share my idea for the book and request a read of a draft of the manuscript. His approval and suggestions were validation that this story was noteworthy and needed to be shared. Not only did he give me the opportunity to become part of a research team focusing on molecular genomics in diseases of African Americans, but he also facilitated my joint appointment to Cooperative Extension where I gained invaluable knowledge of programs and history. Both of those opportunities led to increased personal scientific knowledge and work on projects that contributed to community health. I am eternally thankful to him for affording me these opportunities.

To my sister of a different mother, Dr. Marceline Egnin, I am forever in your debt. Your friendship of many years, beginning with accepting me as a member of your research team, facilitating our trips to Africa to teach molecular genomics, including me in your personal family, and support in all aspects of this manuscript, including participating in our panel presentation of the early outline at the Georgia Historical Association meeting three years ago, has made it possible to me to be able to tell this story. By agreeing to write the Afterword, you link the continuation of Carver's research in his time to today's Agricultural research at Tuskegee University, thus making the story complete. My deepest thanks go to you for being by my side during these years, and especially during this effort.

To my friend, Safari buddy, roommate, and colleague, Carol Harrison, I owe heartfelt gratitude for her loyal support of this story, as well as for her hours of intense review and checking for the accuracy of transcription of the letters selected for inclusion in the manuscript.

My colleague and friend, Dr. James McSwain, must be thanked since he dropped his personal research and dug deeper into his own sources for information on Tom Huston's business efforts prior to establishing the Tom Huston Peanut Company. Jim uncovered the specifics on Huston's manufacturing company where he designed, produced, and sold his plows, skidders, and other farming equipment to a worldwide market. An original member of our infamous "Gang of Five," and an excellent researcher himself, Jim has uncanny skills at finding the most hidden of details that provide added depth to a manuscript. I am grateful for his assistance.

Another person that deserves my profound thanks is my friend, Tom Franklin. I met Tom, husband of Lynn Pearson, my beautiful Auburn High School classmate, several years ago and came to know that he is a skilled gardener. Two years ago, when I was trying to find a peanut plant that actually had flowers, because I needed a good close-up for the book, and, after riding around for hours in Daphne and Macon County, I realized that I had missed that part of the growing season. Dr. Egnin and I had photographed parts of the peanut plant many months earlier from her research plot at Tuskegee University but were not able to get satisfactory pictures of the few flowers that remained. So, to be able to get quality photographs of the flower, I decided to grow my own plants. I recruited Tom to be my backup. After my peanut seeds sprouted, and I transferred them to pots, I halved them with Tom. If mine died or were eaten by a varmint, I would have Tom's as a backup. As it turned out, we were both successful and quality photographs were achieved. Tom also read a later draft of the manuscript and was able to suggest areas that needed clarification and strengthening.

As a member of the "old school," I do not work well from a computer screen when editing hundreds of pages. Over the years I find that I feel more in control if I have a hard copy to work from. To help me keep track of the suggested edits from my publisher, the staff at McQuick's Printing in Auburn were always there to make sure I had the latest copy in the shortest turn-around-time. I literally could not have made the deadlines without the consistent help of John Crenshaw, Lori Ullery, and Haley Jones. Beside their friendship and professional knowledge, they also offered great guidance related to graphics and quality of photographs. They are simply the best! Thanks also to Sarah G. Williams for compiling the index.

To the guys at Cameragraphics, Auburn, John Oliver, owner, Bryan Peters, graphic designer, J. R. and other staff, for the many hours of assistance with quality of photographs, and for helping me divert panic attacks by finding what I consistently managed to lose somewhere in the insides of the computer.

Sincere appreciation to Theresa Ryals, my dental hygienist at Dr. Steve Shriver's office, Opelika, for sharing my story with her mother, Tommie Clegg, and aunt, Margaret Turner, who worked at the Tom Huston Peanut Company for many years. Not only did they graciously contribute memories of their time of employment many years ago with permission to include in the story, but Mrs. Clegg contributed artefacts to become part of a special collection at the Tuskegee University Archives.

I owe an enormous debt of gratitude to Randall Williams and Suzanne La Rosa of NewSouth Books. Randall's "Lazarus Report" describing his recovery from a life-threatening fall requiring a recovery period of several months was received shortly after I signed and returned my contract for publication of my manuscript. Those months were a scary time. Then the COVID-19 pandemic became real. Another scary time and NewSouth Books faced a real challenge to stay on publication schedule. Randall asked his friend Joel Sanders to co-edit and work with me. Joel was a blessing. His skill at quickly picking out the rough spots and his suggestions made the manuscript much better. I am very grateful for his editorial guidance. My heartfelt thanks go also to Suzanne for her suggestions for the cover and ways to improve the final product. It has been a genuine pleasure to be able to work with this honest, caring, and professional group of people. My heart is happy!

A Reader's Note

BERT HITCHCOCK
Professor Emeritus, Auburn University

O nce upon a time, in the Deep, and deeply segregated, South of the United States, there were two men.

Edith Powell has found an extraordinary story to tell. Both the story itself and the circumstances of its discovery are, in some respects, mythic. The relationship of Tom Huston and George Washington Carver is historical fact, however, and its full narration truly inspiring.

Born in the 1800s, Carver being the older by about twenty-five years, both of these men cut a broad swath through their respective callings in the modern twentieth century. Both were persons of exceptional intellect, energy, perseverance, and vision. Each stood out impressively among his contemporaries—a veritable Olympian. Or if not superhuman, clearly "a man among men," as the old dated saying goes. Deservedly (as this book illustrates), Carver's renown has endured. A figure of almost mythic stature, he holds a firm place in the American pantheon. Relatively, the famed reputation of "Tom's Toasted Peanuts" was short-lived. Tom Huston, however, more than merits renewed recognition for his individual personal accomplishments, which included but were not limited to the vital, opportunity-making role he played in Carver's life.

If not quite so classically mythic, how the facts of the entire Huston-Carver story came to light is at least the stuff of popular wishful legend: the unexpected discovery of great riches in some long-ignored place. What may be found at the bottom of that old dusty, musty trunk in a cobwebbed attic, for instance. In this case there were old letters in dusty archives, but not the single breath-sucking item of a bag of gold or lost poem or unknown brilliant book manuscript. It took Edith Powell to fit many letters and artifacts together and realize the historic treasure that existed there.

What began between two men, never having met in person, as a consulting arrangement business deal grew into a remarkable mutually advantageous, mutually respectful, widely consequential partnership. Born out of Huston's recognition that greater scientific knowledge was needed in order to improve the commercial production and profitability of his company, Huston's arrangement with Carver certainly accomplished his goal as well as benefitting Carver—and ultimately many other people. Although Huston personally would lose control of his flourishing peanut enterprise in 1932, beneficiaries of the original two-person agreement would grow greatly in extent and number. Significant scientific knowledge was advanced, and a panoply of institutional, professional, social, and personal gains was achieved. Agricultural research and cooperative Extension services on the national, state, and local levels profited directly, for example, and lives of struggling farm families were improved. The effects were, indisputably, worldwide, still in global evidence today economically and otherwise.

There was as well—and this is what I am most struck by—deep genuine friendships developed in the wake of Carver's inspiring work—transformative change in individuals who found themselves (sometimes quite reluctantly) interacting personally and professionally with "the Doctor." More people should learn the "lesson," one white businessman wrote to Carver, that "the man within is greater than his skin": "I will always consider you one of my best friends." During a time in national and regional American history known more for extreme, negative, often violent racial disconnection, one obscure two-person venture into interracial cooperation, originally an exercising of good business judgment in the face of strong social taboo, had unusually bountiful fruition.

More Than Peanuts is, then, a remarkable story of a pair of remarkable men, individuals of different races but shared humanity, integrity, courage, and good will. I am reminded of the starkly self-descriptive title of a nationally published 1936 book by Alabama author James Saxon Childers: *A Novel About a White Man and a Black Man in the Deep South*. Edith Powell's well-researched book is not a novel, is not fiction.

More Than Peanuts

1

An Unlikely Partnership

It was Tom's idea that a better salted peanut could be made that it could be distributed more efficiently through the existing channel of trade and brought to the consumer with dependable freshness; and that if he performed this service he would reap a suitable reward. Thus in 1925 the Tom Huston Peanut Company was organized.
—"A Peanut Romance"[1]

Tom Huston had a vision of developing a unique process for roasting, and commercially distributing, a salted peanut. However, he had encountered a potentially fatal problem that must be solved if he was to be successful, that of sustaining freshness after packaging. The first step, in 1924, was to establish a partnership with George Washington Carver of the Tuskegee Institute (now University) Department of Agriculture in Tuskegee, Alabama. Hundreds of letters and other correspondence between Tom Huston and two of his employees (Robert Barry and Grady Porter) and Carver are found in the papers of George Washington Carver located in the Tuskegee University Archives. They provide a fascinating account of the vision of Tom Huston and the follow-through by this unlikely team of hand-picked men, three white and one black, from different backgrounds and standings, who worked tirelessly together for five years. Even more astonishing is that, even during this period of intense segregation in the deep South, this work occurred, ensuring that Huston's vision was brought to spectacular fruition.

FROM FARM BOY TO INVENTOR AND CAPITALIST

Despite all of his successes, Tom Huston never liked to be in the public eye. He was shy, reclusive, and humble. The oldest of ten children,[2] Huston was born in 1889 in rural Shelby County, Alabama, about twenty miles outside of Birmingham. While he was still a youngster, his father, Ernest, a descendant of a proud old clan of Scotland, moved Tom's family to a farm near Henderson, Texas, where peanuts were raised as an insurance crop to offset the losses due to the devastating effect of the boll weevil on cotton production. Tom had very few educational advantages to help him on his way to success. Yet, his intense motivation to invent machinery that would make shelling peanuts easier propelled him to his many accomplishments, including becoming a millionaire by his early thirties.[3] According to his brother,

> Tom was an inventor all his life. He was always full of ideas even when they were together on a sandy, stumpy hillside farm in East Texas. Tom invented so many fool contraptions that the neighbors laughed. Tom had grit enough until he could chuckle quietly at the jokesters. He worked at his fool notions at night when the rest of the family slept and in the day, when other folks were fishing or loafing.[4]

On rainy days on the farm, Tom's job was to shell peanuts. This had to be done by hand, a chore Tom quite disliked. So, to make his job easier, he began to design a machine that would do the shelling for him, modeled after corn shelling devices he had seen and used in Texas.[5] Later, Huston said,

> Many a night I've gone to bed with fingers feeling as if they had been held against an emery wheel. This acute discomfort led me to think of a machine which would shell the peanuts. And finally in 1912, after having discarded a number of models, I made a machine that worked satisfactorily.

He said he obtained a patent and then

> arranged with a foundry in Columbus, Georgia, to do the manufacturing and moved up from Texas to be near the scene of operation.[6]

Other than that statement, there is little additional information to indicate why Huston chose to move to Columbus rather than, for instance, Birmingham, which was nearer to his birthplace. Birmingham certainly

Left: Tom Huston (Courtesy of Columbus State University Archives).
Right: The first peanut sheller invented by Huston. The writing on this
side says "Tom Huston Peanut Sheller, Made by Tom Huston, Henderson,
Texas. Pat. Apr. 4, 1916." The reverse side says "Thomas Huston No. 1."

had an abundance of railways, steel refineries, and labor. Perhaps he did
not believe that Birmingham was as progressive a city. Columbus also had
railways and waterways to support its abundant manufacturing, ironworks,
and textile mills. Columbus was a growing, diversified city. Probably a more
compelling reason is that the area surrounding Columbus was primarily rural. The soil was sandy, loamy, and conducive to growing peanuts.
Farmers of the day were searching for crops to replace the cotton losses
caused by the boll weevil. Money was scarce. The United States was in a
world war and the boll weevil was rampant. Huston was surely aware of
these effects on the economy and was searching for a place that would be a
good fit: one that would improve the economic outlook, while offering an
environment of support for his entrepreneurial ideas.[7] Indeed, in an article
located in the Columbus State University archives with no author or date,
Tom Huston is quoted as saying that he came to Columbus, which was
the center of an extensive peanut raising industry, because he decided that

there were not enough peanut growers in Texas to warrant his making the shellers commercially.

About 1918, he occupied his own factory in North Highlands, a historic former village (now a neighborhood in Columbus) whose western side borders the Chattahoochee River, on Thirtieth Street between Second and Third avenues. The resulting Tom Huston Manufacturing Company built the small hand-cranked peanut shellers as well as other farm machines like disc plows, skidders, blades, and stump pullers used in the logging industry. When the need for a bigger, industrial-type machine that could harvest the peanuts on a larger scale became evident, Huston designed one. However, he realized that neither the machine nor the parts would soon wear out, so he could not grow rich from sales. Ironically, despite his success, he now found himself without a job.

Huston had an idea for developing and distributing a dependably fresh and tasty peanut product as his next venture. He had been experimenting for several years with different varieties of peanuts and multiple methods of preparation to find the exact one that would be acceptable to the public and generate return business.[8] With the help of George Washington Carver, Huston had apparently solved the problem of maintaining freshness in the packaged peanuts.

In 1925, with three employees [at this time, the names of the three are not known], in a two-room wooden house on Fourth Avenue in Columbus, behind the

Another peanut sheller displayed at Tom's Foods in Columbus. Painted on the front is "Tom Huston Peanut Sheller. Made by Tom Huston Mfg. Co., Columbus, Georgia."

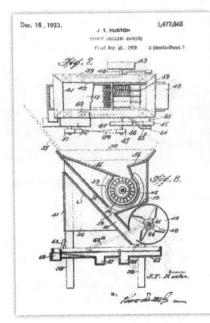

Medley Manufacturing Co., which earlier had manufactured his power-drive shellers, he started shelling and packaging peanuts for sale under the name of "The Tom Huston Peanut Company."

Huston designed an attractive glassine package for his roasted nuts and patented the "famous red triangular label and the trade name 'Tom's Toasted Peanuts.'"

Next, he designed a unique, clear display jar which would be placed by the cash register, filled with the bags of nuts to tempt customers to part

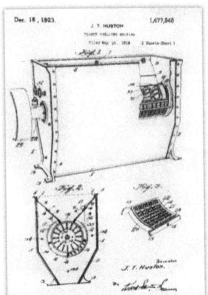

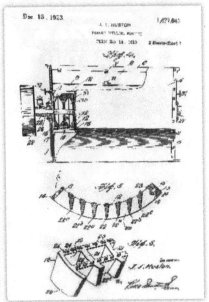

1923 patent drawings for the motor-driven "Tom Huston Floor Model Peanut Sheller commercial peanut sheller." (Courtesy of Columbus State University Archives)

with their nickels.[9] Huston's creative genius was "point of sales advertising" by which he would lure the customers. He designed catchy slogans on display cards which were placed next to the display jar. He also devised a variety of contests which offered cash prizes. The slogans and the contests were his favorite way to advertise.[10]

Huston's 1925 two-room peanut company building in Columbus, Georgia.

Below, the trademark registration Huston filed with the U.S. Patent Office.

Right, the logo Huston created for his company.

Registered Sept. 30, 1930   **Trade-Mark 275,675**

Renewed Sept. 30, 1950, to Tom Huston Peanut Company, of Columbus, Ga.

...ED STATES PATENT OFFICE

...OM HUSTON PEANUT COMPANY, OF COLUMBUS, GEORGIA

ACT OF FEBRUARY 20, 1905

Application filed March 25, 1930. Serial No. 297,865.

Tom's

STATEMENT

To the Commissioner of Patents:

Tom Huston Peanut Company, a corporation duly organized under the laws of the State of Georgia, and located at Columbus, Georgia, and doing business at Eighth Street and Ninth Avenue, Columbus, Georgia, has adopted and used the trade-mark shown in the accompanying drawing, for PEANUTS, SALTED PEANUTS, BUTTERSCOTCH PEANUTS, CHOCOLATE PEANUTS, PEANUT BUTTER, PEANUT BUTTER SANDWICHES AND MALTED-MILK SANDWICHES, in Class 46, Foods and ingredients of foods, and presents herewith five (5) specimens showing the trade-mark as actually used by applicant upon the goods, and requests that the same be registered in the United States Patent Office in accordance with the act of February 20, 1905, as amended.

The trade mark has been continuously used and applied to said goods in applicant's and predecessor's business since April 7, 1925. Applicant is the owner of registrations No. 233,233 and No. 268,717.

The trade mark is applied or affixed to the goods, or to the packages containing the same, by placing thereon a printed label on which the trade mark is shown, or by printing the trade mark on the packages and/or labels.

The undersigned hereby appoints Harold Hirsch, J. Madden Hatcher, and Browne & Phelps, a firm composed of Francis L. Browne and Dudley Browne, as its attorneys, to prosecute this application for registration, with full power of substitution and revocation, and to make alterations and amendments therein, to receive the certificate and to transact all business in the Patent Office connected therewith.

                    TOM HUSTON PEANUT COMPANY,
                    By TOM HUSTON,
                    President.

Within four years, Huston's bags of peanuts were a familiar sight in stores, displayed in glass jars bearing changeable slogans. (Courtesy of Columbus State University Archives)

Huston wrote many of the slogans, such as "They make hunger a joy," "Take no risk—they are fresh and crisp," and "A Meal in a Minute." Some had themes connected to seasonal events, such as newspaper ads with the heading "No Christmas Stocking Is Complete Without a Bag of Tom's." The focus of advertising had shifted in the 1920s. No longer just straight facts about products, advertising became an art form of persuading people to buy things.[11]

HUSTON'S USE OF independent distributors[12] played a huge part in the growing success of the company. His sales representatives bought trucks and filled them with Tom's Peanuts products (changed weekly to ensure freshness) which they set up in counter displays or on free-standing floor shelves in the stores in their districts. The company and the owner-salesmen grew financially successful together. The rapid growth and the story of the farm boy who made good provided great stories for the press, so the Tom's Peanut Company continued its phenomenal growth.

Due to the success of his company, Huston became aware that his glassine package with the red label, the jar container, and his other ideas were being copied by other companies. Huston had to constantly guard his products, the containers, and the product names. Several times he had to initiate legal action against copyright infringement. After the courts consistently found in his favor the illegal activity ceased.

Above, example of a Tom's distributor's truck in the 1920s.
(Courtesy of Columbus State University Archives)

Huston knew that if he expected continued expansion, he needed more peanuts, therefore he had to recruit more peanut growers. He also knew that more peanuts coming into the plant would require more space, so he contracted with Charlie Frank Williams to help establish a second plant

on Thirteenth Street in Columbus. It was a larger building which he then enlarged twice, but still needed additional room.[13]

In 1927, an even larger plant was built on the corner of Eighth Street and Tenth Avenue, a few blocks from his original, small, wooden two-room house. "It was one-eighth of a mile long and contained four hundred workers and dozens of ingenious machines."[14] Located in the southeastern section of the city, it remains in place today, although expanded to occupy the entire city block.

In 1928, Huston incorporated the Tom Huston Peanut Co., which marketed in the United States and other countries. Stock in the company was listed on Wall Street's Curb Market, now the American Exchange. By 1929, Huston's annual gross sales were $2.5 million.[15] Huston rejected an offer of $4 million in October 1929 by a New York syndicate to buy his business. At that time, his plant had four hundred employees and his sales covered twenty states.[16]

Around 1929, with the Tom Huston Peanut Company in excellent financial condition, Huston invested in the quick freezing of fruits, specifically peaches. He was the first person to do so, and he used Tom's Peanut Company as collateral to establish a plant in Montezuma, Georgia. Unfortunately, the available technology was not yet adequate for retail stores to

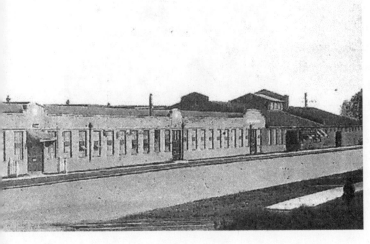

The company's new, larger production facility in Columbus, 1927. (Courtesy of Columbus State University Archives)

cool and store the items once delivered. As a result of this failed venture, coupled with the Great Depression, Huston could not meet a bank note deadline. He lost the Tom Huston Peanut Company in 1932.

FROM SLAVE TO SCIENTIST

George Washington Carver was born a slave on a white-owned farm in Newton County in southwest Missouri. Moses Carver, at age twenty-five, had established the farm with his brother, Richard, after migrating there from Ohio and Illinois in 1837. Two other brothers, Solomon and George, joined them. Moses was able to purchase four adjoining tracts of 240 acres, select an excellent site with plenty of water, and build a rough one-room cabin with one window, a fireplace, and a dirt floor. The cabin was constructed with logs cut from the property.[17] The little settlement community grew during the next twenty years and was called Diamond Grove.

George, who had been widowed prior to moving to Missouri, and one of his daughters died in the same month, leaving another girl and two boys. Moses and his wife, Susan, took in George's children and raised them for fifteen years.

The Moses Carver farm also grew. By 1853 it produced corn, wheat, oats, potatoes, hay, and cattle. Oxen were used to plow the fields and vegetable garden. In addition, Moses maintained an orchard and beehives. By 1855, George's children had

This bronze statue at the George Washington Carver National Monument in Diamond, Missouri, is an artist's imagining of Carver as a boy. (Courtesy of Wikipedia Commons)

The 1881 Moses Carver farm house that replaced the earlier cabin where George Washington Carver lived as a youth. (Courtesy of Wikipedia Commons)

grown up and moved out on their own. Moses and Susan, both now in their fifties, needed help on the farm, so on October 9, 1855, Moses purchased a thirteen-year-old slave girl, Mary, from a neighbor for $700. Four years later, Mary's son, Jim, was born.[18] A new, larger cabin was built for the Carvers, and Mary and Jim lived in the old cabin. Mary gave birth to George in 1864 or 1865. George did not know his father, although he was, according to author Christina Vella in *George Washington Carver: A Life*, a slave owned by a Mr. Grant, the same neighbor who had sold Mary to the Carvers.[19]

Near the end of the Civil War, the Carver farm was attacked and raided by bushwhackers. Jim and Susan Carver had time to hide and were safe, but Mary and baby George were kidnapped. Moses paid his neighbor, John Bentley, to search for them, but only George was found and returned. Mary was never seen again.

Young George had pneumonia and was not expected to live.[20] The Carvers moved the two brothers into their cabin and raised them as their own. Jim grew to be a healthy young man who could help Moses with the chores in the fields (he died in 1883 during a smallpox epidemic).[21] George, however, was a frail, sickly child who was reported to have whooping cough and constant battles with croup. As a result, George mostly helped with the inside chores and was given only light outside work.[22] He had plenty of time to wander outdoors and explore the woods. Early on, despite being darker complexioned than the neighbors, George was labeled as "special" by those who came to know him: "He was too smart, too inquisitive, too observant, and too creative." Because of his ability to nurse sick plants back to health, he became known as the "Plant Doctor."[23]

To this point in his life, George had always lived with white people. He was not familiar with racial prejudice until he and Jim tried to enroll in a school that was taught in the same church building in which they attended services on Sunday.[24] They were denied admission. George did not remember how he learned to read and write, but he did know by heart the old *Webster's Elementary Spelling Book* his mother had given to him. He hungered for more knowledge.[25] Since he could not go to the school in Diamond Grove, he was privately tutored by a young man named Steven Slane. But soon he knew more than Mr. Slane, so the Carvers made arrangements for George to attend a school for blacks in Neosho, Missouri, about eight miles away.[26]

George was about twelve years old when he left the only home and family he had known to begin his long and arduous journey for an education. In Neosho, he met Mariah and Andrew Watkins, a black couple, and he lived with them in their home and helped out with chores. Mariah was a midwife and had a knowledge of medicinal herbs, which she taught to George. A stern and deeply religious woman who did not permit anyone to be wasteful of time or resources, Mariah was well liked by the white community.[27]

George was disheartened to learn that the teacher in his new school knew little more than he did. He had held such high hopes for beginning his "real education." He hitched a ride to Fort Scott, Kansas, where he found a job to earn money to continue his search for education. It was here that George witnessed a heinous act that he never forgot: a black man, accused of raping a white female, was pulled from the jail, dragged through the streets with a rope around his neck, then hanged from a lamp post.[28] George was so terrified that he moved immediately to Olathe, Kansas. He lived there with Lucy and Ben Seymour and helped Lucy in her laundry business. He lived with the Seymours for several more years. During this period, he continued

Studio photograph of Carver as a teenager in Kansas. (Courtesy of Tuskegee University Archives)

to develop his artistic skills: music, drawing and painting, sewing, knitting, and crocheting.[29]

Deciding to try formal education again, he applied to and was accepted at a small Presbyterian college in Highland, Kansas. But when he arrived, he was told that there had been a mistake, and he could not attend after all. It is hard to tell the color of one's skin by reading an application form.[30] Carver was so disappointed that he gave up the idea of school. In 1886, he moved to Beeler, Kansas, where he purchased a quarter-section of land and became a sod farmer.[31]

Two years later, he was ready to continue his quest for an education. In 1888, he left Kansas and went to Winterset, Iowa, where he met the white Milhollands. Thus came the first big break that would lead Carver to his life's work. He had opened a laundry and began to attend the local churches. Mrs. Milholland heard him singing in the choir and asked to meet him. She persuaded Carver to apply to a nearby Methodist school, Simpson College, which he did and was accepted. At Simpson, he was well received, worked hard, and made many friends.[32]

Carver excelled in his art classes taught by Miss Etta Budd. When he shared his life-long interest in plants, she persuaded him to change schools. She suggested that he switch his major from art to botany, so that he could graduate with a degree that would offer him a much better chance for quality, life-supporting job opportunities. In 1891, Carver transferred to Iowa State College of Agriculture and Mechanical Arts.[33] He became the first and only black student on campus.[34] There he received the friendship and assistance of men who would go on to become leaders at the highest level of the United States government.[35] Carver's instructors at Iowa State, James Wilson and Henry C. Wallace, became Secretaries of Agriculture, as did Wallace's son, Henry A. Wallace. As an adult, Henry A. Wallace, a future vice president of the United States, would tell the story of how when he was a little boy Carver took him out into the fields and taught him about plants and fertilization.[36] Prior to becoming vice president, Wallace established the Hi-Bred Corn Company (later the Dupont-Pioneer-Dow conglomerate).

Carver at Iowa State College. (Courtesy of Tuskegee University Archives)

During his time at Iowa State, Carver participated in religious activities, the YMCA, and campus clubs. He helped organize the Agricultural Society, and he not only played the guitar at the meetings of the Welsh Eclectic Society but gave dramatic and humorous readings as well. In addition, Carver became the rubber, or masseur, for the Iowa State football team. His outstanding skills and knowledge, developed as part of his coursework in mycology and plant breeding, brought recognition by his peers as well as by faculty. After completing his undergraduate degree, he was accepted into the graduate program to continue his research and was also assigned freshman biology courses to teach. While in graduate school, Carver published three articles and added several hundred mycological specimens to the college's collection.[37]

George Carver had always been a very spiritual person. Believing that God gave him the talents he possessed, he never forgot to be grateful for those gifts. Over the years, he had developed a gentle, quiet personality. While at Iowa State, he was totally focused on his work; he arose at four each morning and took walks to "talk with God about his day." He then went to his office and either worked in his laboratory, taught classes, or inspected the greenhouses. He enjoyed teaching. He worked tirelessly, stopping for dinner, which he might cook for himself in his room, and then reading the Bible or answering correspondence until his 9 p.m. bedtime.[38]

ON APRIL 2, 1896, CARVER wrote to Booker T. Washington, principal of Tuskegee Institute in Alabama, and expressed his interest in working among his people, the poor black farmers, many of whom were former slaves, who lived throughout the region. In May, Washington offered Carver a position to be assumed upon the completion of his coursework at Iowa State in the fall of that year. Carver had declined a previous job offer with Alcorn Agricultural and Mechanical College in Mississippi but accepted Washington's invitation. Perhaps his decision was made after hearing about Washington's Atlanta Exposition speech in 1895, wherein Washington outlined his philosophy of "accommodation." He stated that, if "African Americans wanted to gain economic independence, they should cast down their buckets where they were, learn to support themselves and their families, and accept the South's racial caste system until they had proven themselves worthy of social uplift."[39] When accepting the position at Tuskegee, Carver wrote to Washington, "it has always been the one ideal of my life to be of the greatest good to the greatest number of 'my people' possible and to this end I have been preparing myself for these many years; feeling as I do that this line of education is the key to unlock the golden door of freedom to our people."[40] By this time in his life and with the experiences of his journey, Carver had also developed a strong belief in self-help and interracial cooperation. Little did he know how critically these ideals would be taxed as he began his life's work in the South.

Carver arrived on the campus of Tuskegee Institute in October 1896 as the only member of the faculty to hold an advanced degree from a white college. He was to earn an annual salary of $1,000.[41]

Carver began his plot work with peanuts in 1903 (a passion that continued until the publication, a month after his death, of his last bulletin).[42] In the years prior to his partnership with Tom Huston, Carver had developed a reputation as an expert on peanuts. He had a wide range of professional colleagues with whom he regularly corresponded and shared thoughts or

Above, Carver, front row center, on the Tuskegee Institute faculty, 1902. Right, Carver at Tuskegee, 1910. (Courtesy of Tuskegee University Archives)

concerns. Carver's longtime friend, M. M. Osborn, editor of *The Peanut Journal*, a journal that had previously published Carver's work, wrote to Carver in March 1924, to share an observation:

> There is one thing that stands in our way on promoting the Peanut Flour Industry and that is the small production of peanuts in the Southeast, which makes the price of peanuts too high for this product. We must get the farmers in that section to understand how to produce peanuts, and get the most per acre. They do not seem to know how to fertilize and rotate their crops, in growing peanuts, and until they do this they cannot expect to increase their yields per acre.[43]

On May 14, 1924, Carver received a letter from D. Breese Jones, Chemist in Charge, Protein Investigation Laboratory, USDA, Bureau of Chemistry, Washington, D.C., requesting information concerning the inorganic constituents of the peanut, including its sugar and carbohydrate content. Mr. Jones stated that he had done a rather cursory search of the chemical literature and found no related work published. He did not seem to know that Carver had published the same several years earlier.[44]

Such was the state of awareness of the research that was available at the time of Carver's initial letter from Tom Huston, and its relationship to the impact of the following story. Carver's correspondence and work with Huston, Bob Barry, and Grady Porter, of the Tom Huston Peanut Company continued until his death on January 5, 1943.

Carver's work at Tuskegee has been positively documented by Rackham Holt, Linda McMurray, Gary Kremer, Mark Hersey, Peter Burchard, and criticized by others, including Barry McIntosh and Christina Vella. A partial listing of articles/essays written by Carver and published during the time of this story may be found in Appendix B.

THE PEANUT

One might have asked George Washington Carver the same question he said that he had posed to the Great Creator early in his scientific career:

> Then I told the Creator I wanted to know all about the peanut. He replied that my mind was too small to know *all* about the peanut, but He said He would give me a handful of peanuts. And God said, "Behold, I have given you every herb bearing seed, which is upon the face of the earth . . . to you it shall be for meat . . . I have given ever green herb for meat: and it was so." I carried the peanuts into my laboratory and the Creator told me to take them apart and resolve them into their elements. With such knowledge as I had of chemistry and physics I set to work to take them apart. I separated them into water, the fats, the oils, the gums, the resins, sugars, starches, pectoses, pentosans, amino acids. There! I had the parts of the peanuts all spread out before me. I looked at Him and He looked at me. "Now, you know what the peanut is."

"Why did you make the peanut?" The Creator said, "I have given you three laws; namely, compatibility, temperature, and pressure. All you have to do is take these constituents and put them together, observing these laws, and I will show you why I made the peanut." I therefore went on to try different combinations of the parts under different conditions of temperature and pressure, and the result was what you see.[45]

The Great Creator provided directions, and Carver went into his laboratory. And from his findings he shared many answers, in written, verbal, and demonstration forms.

If one has never seen a peanut plant, the next question might be: What does the peanut plant look like? In spite of its name, the peanut is not a nut, but a legume: *Arachis hypogaea*. It was named by the botanist Linnaeus to describe the atypical growing pattern of the plant's seeds which develop underground rather than aboveground (*hypogaea* meaning "under the earth"). This unique characteristic is in addition to, and not part of, the normally expected root system. Also interesting is the fact that the peanut has the capability to fix nitrogen in nodules located along the underground tap root system, making it require less nitrogen-containing fertilizer, while improving soil fertility, which is valuable to the concept of crop rotation.[46]

The peanut is a plant of the legume, or pea, family and its seed form in pods. Peanut plants grow to just over one foot in height and spread about three feet [depending on type]. The leaves are very green, and the flowers are bright yellow flowers. Peanut plants are self-pollinating, meaning that both male and female flowers appear on the same plant. Once the flowers wilt, the flower stalk (called a peg) grows down into the ground about an inch deep, where its ovary develops into pods containing the nuts, or seeds. Once the seeds mature, they can be harvested. Harvesting is a two-part process. First, a digger with a four-to-six inch horizontal blade is driven down the rows. This loosens the plants from the root while a shaker lifts and inverts it, exposing the pods to sunlight. Once the pods dry out for a few days, a combine or thresher cuts the pods from the vines, places the pods in a hopper on top of the machine, and replaces the vines and stems on the ground where they serve as moisture-retaining mulch.

A Spanish peanut plant, with nitrogen nodules on the underground tap root, and peanuts at various stages of growth attached to the pegs above ground. Photograph taken from the booklet, Peanuts: Culture and Marketing of the White Spanish Variety in the Southeastern States, *2nd Edition, 1931, published by the Tom Huston Peanut Company.*

The harvested pods are then placed in drying containers to cure, reducing their moisture content to around 10 percent.

Peanuts thrive in warm, subtropical climates and in sandy, well-drained chalky soils, both attributes of the southern states. Shelled raw peanuts, which are the plant's seeds, are planted after the last spring frost when the soil temperature reaches around 65 [degrees Fahrenheit], usually in March or April. Harvesting takes place in September or October, anywhere from 120–160 days after planting. Peanuts are a dual crop, grown for both the nut itself and peanut hay.

Four major types of peanuts are grown in the United States: runner, Spanish, Valencia, and Virginia. Runner peanuts are grown mostly in Alabama, Georgia, Florida, Texas, and Oklahoma. They are used to make peanut butter and candy or sold as roasted snack nuts. Spanish peanuts, a smaller, rounder variety with a higher oil content are grown primarily in Oklahoma and Texas, and are used to make candies, peanut butter, and peanut oil, and are sold as snack nuts. Valencia peanuts, which are grown mostly in New Mexico, have a bright red skin and feature three to four and sometimes even five nuts per shell. Their sweet flavor makes them ideal for boiled peanuts. Virginia peanuts feature the largest peanut kernels of all the varietals and are most commonly used as snack nuts or roasted in the shell.[47]

Prior to 2014, Peru or Brazil was believed to be origin of the peanut. Although no fossil records have been found to prove this theory, pottery in the shape of peanuts has been found among the people of South America from as far back as 3,500 years ago. *Arachis hypogaea* does not grow wild. It is the hybrid, cultivated peanut that we know today. The question of the relationships of the wild species to cultivated peanut has long been of interest to researchers: if this is a hybrid, then where did the original peanut plant come from? How did it get to the U.S.? As of 2014, the answer to the first question is now available. Scientists working with the Peanut Genome Project, organized in 2004, report that "the ancestors of today's modern peanut can be found around 8,000 BC in the Andean mountains, and they're still the spitting image of their 10,000-year-old ancestor, the hybrid of *Arachis duranensis*a wild herb native to Argentina, Bolivia, and

Paraguay, and *Arachis ipaensis*, native to Bolivia."[48] To accomplish that goal of the Peanut Genome Project, the original plant(s) had to be found and identified and their DNA sequenced and compared to the DNA of the peanut of today. The results of the research findings are summarized in the following report:

> Scientists have long speculated that the genetic material in cultivated peanut (*Arachis hypogaea*) is a hybrid derived from two separate plant species, *Arachis duranesis*, a native herb in the Andean mountains, [in South America] and *Arachis ipaensis*, a cousin of the modern peanut. They believe that early inhabitants of South America brought *A. ipaensis* into the area where *duranensis* was naturally growing, and the two species cross-pollinated to create peanuts. As a result, peanuts inherited chromosomes from both of these plant species. Mapping the peanut genome, therefore, meant that scientists first needed to map these two "parent" species. Complicating that process was the fact that until recently, scientists thought *A. ipaensis* was extinct.
>
> All of that changed when researchers from the University of Georgia discovered that *A. ipaensis* was alive and well and growing in Bolivia. Not only were they able to confirm that *A. duranensis* and *A. ipaensis* were in fact the original species that gave birth to the peanut, but they also discovered through mapping the DNA of those species, that peanuts today remain 99.96 percent identical to their ancient progenitor.[49]

To answer to the second question, the peanut's route to the U.S. began when European explorers discovered tribes in Brazil making a drink by grinding peanuts with maize. The Incas in Peru entombed peanuts with mummies as sacrificial offerings to aid in the journey to their spiritual afterlife. When the Spanish began exploring the New World, they found peanuts growing as far north as Mexico. They took them back to Spain, and from there the peanut journeyed through Asia and Africa. Peanuts were brought to America by African slaves in the 1700s. The Africans had grown them abundantly in their home countries, and referred to them as "goobers" which comes from the Congo name for peanuts—*nguba*, also as "ground peas," or, inaccurately, as "ground nuts."[50] They became very popular during the Civil War, especially with Confederate soldiers. When the Union soldiers took them back home, they found that, although the peanut itself did not grow well in the cold, northern climate, their popularity did and spread throughout the North. According to available records, peanuts were not grown as a commercial crop in the U.S. until the early 1800s. First planted in Virginia, the peanut continued its journey southward and westward.

Their popularity grew when, in the late 1800s, drivers of P. T. Barnum's circus wagons traveling across the country called out "hot roasted peanuts!" to the crowds. Street vendors began selling roasted peanuts from carts and soon shifted the preference from boiled to "hot roasted peanuts" as they were made available to the public. (No one knows exactly when or why Southerners started boiling peanuts, although, since peanuts were brought over with African slaves, who commonly boiled and roasted peanuts in their daily diets, it is likely that the practice of boiling peanuts with a little salt began during the Colonial period.)[51] Their popularity increased as their availability spread to America's favorite sport, baseball, beginning when Harry Stevens decided to sell advertising space on the games' scorecards to a peanut company.[52] But rather than pay for the ads in cash, the company paid in peanuts, and then these peanuts were sold in the ballpark. This was in 1895, when the "peanut gallery" spectators in the cheap seats munched volumes of the inexpensive food. Later, the song "Take Me Out to the Ballgame," written in 1908, served to continually remind everyone to enjoy the tasty snack while at the game.[53]

Although the peanut was increasing in popularity during the early 1900s, commercial production was still being done by hand. This process left stems and trash in the product, which affected the quality of the product as evidenced by reduced demand and slow sales.[54]

While the folks in Washington wrestled with responding to nationwide demands for farm assistance, in the South cotton growers faced devastating losses caused by the Mexican boll weevil, which had crossed into Texas in the 1890s and had steadily eaten its way eastward across the U.S., arriving in southeast Alabama about 1909–1910. The weevil was decimating the South's cotton crop, and George Washington Carver, in 1903, in his little laboratory at Tuskegee Institute began focusing his research on the peanut. Previously, in the late 1800s, he had been experimenting with ways to improve cotton, publishing Bulletin No. 3, *Fertilizer Experiments on Cotton* in 1899, followed by Bulletins Nos. 6 and 7 (1905), 14 (1908), and 20 (1911). In his bulletin, *Growing Cotton for Rural Schools* published in 1911, Carver warned of the threat of the Mexican boll weevil: although not in Macon County yet, it "is in the state and moving this way rapidly."[55]

Carver appreciated the total damage that this weevil could cause, and he recognized that this would be the end of cotton as the "one product of the South." Since cotton continually grown in the same field depletes the soil of essential nutrients, it was critical for the development of alternative crops that first the quality of the soil be improved.[56]

Carver began encouraging both sharecroppers and plantation owners to grow peanuts using the method of crop rotation to replenish the worn-out soil; the harvested peanuts would serve as a potential cash crop to replace cotton losses. Unfortunately, although the peanut crops grew, the market did not. Carver also began his peanut plot research in 1903[57] so that, during the annual Farmer's Conferences at Tuskegee University, he could demonstrate the growing plants and discuss the cultivation methods.[58] Simultaneously, he was visiting the farmers in their fields and promoting the peanut as a replacement crop, or at least, rotating it with cotton.[59] In the laboratory, Carver was breaking the peanut down into its components and publishing his findings of the protein content while extolling its value as the almost perfect food. He published his first bulletin on peanuts in 1916.[60]

MIGRATION PATTERN OF THE BOLL WEEVIL

    1892 Mexico → Texas near Brownsville
        1900 → Louisiana
            1907 → Mississippi in Natchez area
                1914 → Northeast Mississippi
            1909 → Mobile County, Alabama
              1920 → South Carolina
                  1922 → Throughout Eastern cotton-growing states to Virginia

From 1892 to 1922, the boll weevil spread across the South at about 55 miles per year.

In 1920, Carver was invited to make a presentation in Montgomery, Alabama, to the newly organized United Peanut Association. He took his peanut exhibit, which had drawn favorable comments earlier at the Alabama State Fair and demonstrated the many possible commercial products of the peanut, as well as its nutritional value.

During the early 1900s, the farming sector had dramatically expanded. By 1906, the number of farms had tripled, the population living on them had grown, and their value had soared. In the early 1910s, commodity prices rose even further, and by 1914 were the highest in a century. This was known as the "Golden Age" of agriculture. When America became involved in World War I in 1917, prices shot up, and farmers borrowed heavily to buy out neighbors and expand their holdings. The resulting high debt made farmers vulnerable to the coming downturn in agricultural prices. After the war, Europe's agriculture market rebounded; overproduction then resulted in plummeting prices and stagnant market conditions, which led to a lower standard of living for U.S. farmers. Thousands who had borrowed to expand their land holdings now could not meet the financial burden. They demanded relief and federal subsidies. When President Woodrow Wilson, a Democrat, was slow to respond, the Republican Party made political hay. As a result, Warren G. Harding was elected as the next president.

Meanwhile, Alabama farm officials remained so impressed with Carver's 1920 presentation in Montgomery that he was invited to make another trip, this one of significantly more importance to the future of the peanut industry. On January 21, 1921, during efforts to get the Committee to vote for a protective tariff against Chinese and Japanese peanut imports, he testified to the House of Representatives Ways and Means Committee in Washington, D.C., on the importance of the peanut to U.S. agriculture, especially in the South.

Once in office, President Harding responded to the needs of farmers by signing the Emergency Tariff Act of 1921, which provided some relief, and the country saw the beginning of the first large-scale federal intervention in the farm commodities market. This Act was intended to be temporary while giving Congress time to develop a more substantial bill. The resulting Fordney-McCumber Tariff was signed by Harding on September 21,

1922. Harding died in office in 1923 and Vice President Calvin Coolidge succeeded him.

Farm prices steadily worsened in the mid-1920s. A plan based on an equalization fee (parity doctrine) was presented by Senator Charles L. McNary and Representative Gilbert L. Haugen. Although this legislation was before Congress from 1924 to 1928, and passed both houses, Coolidge vetoed it twice in favor of a plan devised by Commerce Secretary Herbert Hoover and Agriculture Secretary William M. Jardine. This plan would modernize farming by bringing in more electricity, more effective equipment, better seeds and breeds, more rural education, and better business practices. It also advocated the creation of a Federal Farm Board. The Hoover plan was adopted in 1929.[61]

Following his 1921 testimony to Congress, which was published by the media nationwide, Carver's reputation grew, and he began to receive requests for peanut information from farmers as well as from commercial producers.[62]

In a January 31, 1924, letter, M. M. Osborn, editor of *The Peanut Journal*, wrote to Carver with an idea to increase the commercial sale of peanuts:

An older Carver in his laboratory at Tuskegee Institute. (Courtesy of Tuskegee University Archives)

I have your very welcome letter of the 28th, and want to thank you for your trouble in supplying me with the information about protein content of Peanuts and

Peanut Products. I have figured out copy for the enclosure, and am going to make announcement of our offer in this respect in February issue. I believe that most of the Peanut people will take onto the proposition, and if they do it will mean a million or more of them as my idea is to furnish them at cost of printing to all mills, and manufactures of peanut products to enclose in every letter and circular they send out.[63]

By 1924, Carver was firmly established as "the Peanut Man."[64] And, Tom Huston had sold his equipment manufacturing business and was now focusing his business acumen on finding ways to increase the total amount of peanuts in the marketplace.

Thus begins our story of the unlikely, unique, enduring partnership of a white entrepreneur and a former slave at a black educational institution entrenched in the middle of the segregated South. Young Tom Huston, who had relocated to Columbus, Georgia, and started his fast-growing company from scratch, had the expertise of the agricultural Extension Service at the University of Georgia in Athens at his disposal, yet he chose George Washington Carver, an older, humble, educated, brilliant black man in a new experimental school located in the small town of Tuskegee, Alabama, to become his partner and the problem-solver to lead his business to the stunning success it would become.

2

The Beginning

*Although the Tom Huston Peanut Company was organized in
1925, several previous years were spent in experimenting with
different varieties of peanuts and methods of preparing them,
in order to get the one that would please the greatest number
of tastes and assure repeat business. A particular small tender,
Spanish peanut and a special toasting process were decided on.
That a correct decision was made is evidenced by the fact that
over a million packages of Tom's are sold each week.*
—"A Peanut Romance"[65]

In a letter dated October 18, 1924, Tom Huston wrote George Carver
that although he had wanted to meet the professor personally, he deeply
regretted that he had not been able to schedule such a meeting. He had been
vitally interested in peanuts for a great many years and had been building
peanut machinery for several years. Getting to his main point, he went on:

> Aside from any interest coming from a machinery standpoint, I have always
> been greatly concerned in the consumption of peanuts. I have always felt that
> there should be many times the amount of peanuts consumed by human be-
> ings as is the case at the present time.
>
> While the consumption of peanut butter has increased to a very great extent
> during the past few years, still there has been only a very small increase in the
> consumption of whole or salted peanuts. A good while ago I concluded this was
> due to two reasons. One reason the sales have not gained is because when a
> person buys a five-cent bag of peanuts from a confectioner's stock he never
> knows whether they are going to be stale or whether they are going to be good

and crisp. And here's the other reason. Regardless of whether they are found to be stale or good and crisp, you can always count on having to wash your hands to remove the oil and salt after you have finished eating them.

I have learned how to keep peanuts from becoming stale almost indefinitely simply by displaying them and keeping the stock in moisture proof containers. Moisture is to a salted peanut as poison gas is to a man.

What I now seek to do is to put the required salty flavor inside the peanut kernel without having to use oil in an effort to stick salt on the outside. With my total lack of knowledge of chemistry, this job is too much for me. I feel, however, that with your knowledge of chemistry together with your knowledge of peanuts will enable you to furnish me a formula. You may probably need to experiment a bit but I presume that you are well equipped for that. I am not asking something for nothing and of course expect to pay for any information or formula that is of value.

I am sending you by parcel post a small amount of exceedingly delicious salted peanuts. There is no way to make them more delicious. The only possible improvement I believe would be to put the salty flavor on the inside of the peanuts instead of sticking the salt on the outside with oil. Now, the process necessary to put the salt on the inside might in some way damage either the flavor, crispness or the keeping qualities of the nut. That is something else that I wish to know.

Yours very truly,

Tom Huston

P.S. It will probably interest you to know that the machinery used in practically all the shelling plants throughout the southeast was designed by me and manufactured by our company.[66]

A short second letter from Huston to Carver was dated the same day:

Prof. Geo. W. Carter [*sic*],
Dear Sir:

In writing you this morning I failed to mention that the peanuts being sent you were prepared in the following manner:

The nuts were roasted sufficiently to loosen the red skins in order that they might be blanched. Then, after the blanching process they were dipped in boiling cocoanut [*sic*] oil to finish the cooking process. After being removed from the oil they were cooled as quickly as possible and then the salt was added.[67]

    Yours very truly,

    Tom Huston

Carver responded in a letter dated October 23, 1924. He acknowledged receipt of Huston's letter and indicated that he read it "with a great deal of interest. In fact with much more interest than usual." He told Huston that he would like to meet with him, but, since they were both scheduled to be traveling out of town for several weeks, a time would have to be set when they returned home. Carver went on:

I am very much interested in what you propose and you have certainly made a great contribution to the industry as this has been one of the greatest. I have received the package of roasted nuts also. The mice had gotten through the package and destroyed one box. I must say they seem to me a most delicious that I have eaten. If you could succeed in getting the oil into the nut, it would be a wonderful addition. I really believe it can be done but will require a great deal of experimental work. I shall be glad to give some attention to this when I can get to it as I am very much interested.

    Thank you for the process you sent me which means that the pores are open as by a slight roasting, then dipping them into the boiling oil which seals the flavor within the nut and makes really a superior product. I certainly congratulate you on it. With sincere good wishes and with the hope that I can be of further service in this splendid work you are doing, I am

    Very truly yours,

    Director of Research and Experiment Station [68]

In a follow-up letter to Carver dated October 25, 1924, Huston wrote:

Mr. Geo. W. Carver,

Tuskegee Institute, Ala.

    Glad to have your interesting letter of October 23rd.

I infer from your letter that you expect to be in attendance at the Montgomery Fair during the entire time from November 3rd to 11th. Is this correct?

I have been planning to make a trip to Montgomery within the next few weeks and think I could very conveniently arrange to be in Montgomery one day during the Fair.

Yours truly,

Tom Huston[71]

In 1924, two years before Huston began marketing peanuts in his innovative cellophane bags, the industry's two greatest promoters met. This was the beginning of "a long and close relationship in which Carver frequently provided advice on new products and visited Huston's summer home on Lake Harding as well as his office on Second Avenue. Carver's experience was so valued, in fact, that in 1929, when the company expanded its research lab, he was formally asked to join Huston's staff."[69]

Meanwhile, correspondence and interactions expanded to others on the staff. A letter from Carver dated April 12, 1926, is addressed to the Tom Huston Peanut Company:

Gentlemen: -Dear Sirs:

I beg to acknowledge receipt of your splendid samples of peanuts which you have so kindly sent me. They came in time to distribute among some very important people indeed, as we had Founders Day yesterday, and the meeting of our Board of Trustees today, and last week a large gathering of the Enter-racial [sic] Commission. Each gathering was very large, and it was a great pleasure to distribute them among the people as far as they would go. It was equally as interesting to hear their comments, which were exactly the same as mine, the best they had ever eaten. I believe this distribution will be of service to the product which it is a pleasure for me to acquaint people with, as its merits speak for themselves.

Again thanking you and feeling very happy over the splendid product you are putting up, I am

Very truly yours

G. W. Carver

Dept. of Research and Experiment Station[70]

In a March 5, 1928, letter to Carver, Huston mentions that he hoped that Carver would have come to Columbus during the previous week. He apprizes Carver that he is leaving for a month-long trip and suggests that Carver not come over until later in the spring.[71]

On July 2, 1928, Carver wrote to Fred A. Woleban at the Tom Huston Peanut Company in response to a previous question [Woleban's letter is not available]:

> You raise some very important questions, and indeed one question that has puzzled scientists for a long time. As far as I know no one has been able to settle the question satisfactorily as yet, that is the rancidity of peanuts. Just what part of the peanut causes it. Much work is being done in this direction . . .

Carver told Woleban that he would have been over to visit earlier, but due to the absence of Huston and the extensive rain creating dangerous road conditions, he would postpone until Huston's return.[72]

In an October 16, 1928, letter, Carver told Huston that he was very happy to see him looking so much better than he expected. Evidently Huston had returned from his trip and had recovered from a serious illness, and he and Carver had finally met after many delays. Carver began his letter:

> My very, very dear Friend Mr. Huston:
>
> Your good letter has delighted me so very much. Nothing could please me more than to know that you were almost well again. I hope with you that you will never have ptomaine poisoning again.
>
> I presume by this time you have received the samples. Mr. Thompson says that I did not get your idea at all with the crystalized nuts. He says you want a sort of glasine or *cellopane* coverings, that is a clear translucent covering.
>
> I crystallized some and used a mint flavor. They are delicious. I am going to try out the walnut flavors, as soon as I can return from the Fair and recover from its effects . . . I see where all sorts of flavors can be had in the crystalized nuts, as well as attractive colors . . .

As I get time to work I shall keep you advised and probably run over for a
conference . . .
Yours with genuine love and admiration,
    G. W. Carver[73]

In this same letter, Carver told Huston that he had spoken with the
peanut company's unnamed chemist on the previous day and assumed that
Mr. Woleban would be bringing the chemist over for a face-to-face meeting.

Although written correspondence seems scarce after the initial contacts
in 1924, the relationship between Huston and Carver continued, most likely
via personal visits and phone conversations. The written letters resumed in
1928, becoming much more frequent in the coming months as the problems Huston faced in 1924 seem to have been solved and the focus of the
arrangement changed to meet new challenges. Carver mentioned in his
October 16, 1928, letter to Huston that "I still consider my week-end visit
with you one of the most pleasant and profitable to me that I have had, as
my vision has been so enlarged."

Huston continued to increase the amount of harvested peanuts coming
into the company, and as a by-product of the increased shelling process,
there was a buildup of the separated peanut skins which were being disposed
of as waste material.

Carver, always looking for ways to reduce waste, advised Huston in an
October 17, 1928, letter that he was sending him a product.

My dear Mr. Huston:
    Under separate cover, I am sending you a product which is self explanatory.
This amount comes from two ounces of peanut skins, just as they were sent to
me, and I presume as they came from the machine. I take it for granted that
this represents the average skins as they come from the machine, if so I am
wondering if these skins are not worth more to you in the way of combinations
which naturally occur from your various manufacturing operations, all of which
are more or less high in food value, high in protein content and in some cases,
sugar. Of course, I do not know just what percentage of sugar waste you have.
When I was there I saw two or three barrels going out as waste to be fed to

hogs, most of which contained high sugar content. This could be worked into a sweet stock food, and with the large pile of waste from the huller, I should think a stock food of value could be made, which would mean more or less to dospose of the skins at $25.00 per ton.

Of course, this is a mere suggestion, and I may be all wrong not having all the facts I ought to have. It is a fine problem, I think, for your chemist to take up.

I am also extracting dyes in which the skins are rather rich at the present. It may be, however, vegetable dyes are not interesting to the dye trade, which does not mean that an interest cannot be worked up or formed for them.

With sincerely good wishes, I am

Very truly yours,

G. W. Carver

Department of Research and Experiment Station[74]

Now that Huston had a new, larger building and space for increased tonnage of peanuts, he realized that he had reached a critical decision point. His original vision of a successful peanut and products distribution business had become a reality and was gaining momentum. Now, he needed a revised business plan focused on the challenges that lay ahead. To remain viable, he knew he needed to continue to increase his inventory of peanuts while addressing serious problems in the industry. He assigned two of his employees, Bob Barry, manager of the Shelling Department, and Grady Porter, field manager, to assist Carver at Tuskegee.

Huston now had a dynamic team. Feeling confident that they would guide his plan to unprecedented success in a short time, he could now focus his attention on the new endeavor of establishing a frozen fruit operation. After he talked over that idea with his team, he charged them with an assignment to be completed in two years. He explained the new plan would include two objectives: (1) an outreach and education strategy to increase the number of growers and (2) a strategy to educate the public about the use of the products. A critical part of the plan was the need to understand and control the diseases being reported by Grady Porter in peanut crops all over Georgia. During the previous months, Porter had been visiting peanut growers and talking with them about their experiences, successes, or problems during the past growing seasons. He had evidence that many of the growers had experienced problems with plant health, and even crop loss, due to apparent disease. These reports revealed a serious situation: there was virtually no information available for the identification or treatment of these diseases. These problems had been discussed among the team, and the potential catastrophic damage to both the growers and the peanut industry had become a major consideration in developing the new plan. As Carver pointed out, the first step had to be to identify the cause-agent; then a control method could be designed. This part of the plan was crucial and would have to involve the USDA scientists in Washington, D.C. Much effort would be required, since, at this point, no one at that level seemed concerned about a peanut problem that could cripple the entire industry. While there were federal funds for problem-solving assistance in other areas of agriculture, at that time no such money was available to the peanut industry and peanut farmers.

To increase and sustain an industry with the commercial potential as large as that of the peanut, two major challenges had to be overcome. First, increasing the number of farmers growing peanuts would be accomplished only by targeted education to increase their awareness of the economic potential and by providing assistance for solving the challenges they would face in growing peanuts. Second, the awareness that there was a major threat to the future viability of the peanut industry had to be recognized by federal leadership so that adequate funding could be provided. Both challenges would require funds, leadership, and manpower, which Tom Huston Peanut Company was willing to provide until the federal funds could be secured.

3

The Plan and the
Ultimate Strategy

The peanut has become almost a universal diet for man . . .
Of all the money crops grown by Macon County farmers,
perhaps there are none more promising than the peanut in its
several varieties and their almost limitless possibilities.
—GEORGE WASHINGTON CARVER, *Bulletin No. 31*[75]

By 1929, the Tom Huston Peanut Company team of Bob Barry and Grady Porter and collaborator George Washington Carver was hard at work on its mission: part one, to grow and sell more peanuts; and part two, to control the diseases that would cripple part one. A trade magazine noted the plan, saying it would "probably be the greatest single effort ever made by Tom to promote the sale of his products."[76]

One key goal was to get federal and state governments to recognize the potential of the peanut industry and support it with appropriations. For months Porter had been collecting diseased plants, so the team knew there were peanut diseases that could wipe out a crop overnight. But it was not known what the diseases were, how widespread the problem was, or how to treat the plants to control and prevent disease. The team did know the work required to identify and control these diseases would be expensive. Huston's group felt that the peanut had the potential to bring millions of dollars to the southeast region, so the crop deserved to be recognized at the federal level as cotton and soybeans were.

A tight scientific approach was needed to identify causes of disease, spread, and treatments. Diseased plants would be sent to Carver for identification and treatment protocol. Carver would share some of his findings with peer researchers for validation, both at Experiment Stations at other universities, and at the USDA. Next, understanding was needed of the impact disease could have on peanut crops. The Tom Huston Peanut Company agreed to fund research and to publish the findings in a disease registry to be made available at the local, state, and national levels. This would be top-priority work during 1930 and 1931. By 1931, the team would have a full year of data and could begin publishing reports. To make it a "show-and-tell," the team invited USDA scientists to join in visits to growers to see for themselves what the diseased crops looked like, learn how critical the problems were, and better understand their economic impact. The USDA scientists would go back and make reports to the government agencies. The Experiment Stations and county agents would also be involved. Meanwhile, the team was conducting its own research on Tom Huston-owned acres. Other researchers at Experiment Stations and universities were invited to set up their own research plots.

The team would then fold in the 1931 growing experiences, totaling enough scientific-based data to present to the targeted decision-makers identified during the information collection. By then the team would also be able to initiate the education-awareness effort by sharing the findings publicly through presentations, targeted mailings, participation in trade association meetings, and exhibits at local and state fairs.

In the second year, the team planned a media blitz of articles in major journals, written by themselves and as many experts as possible. The team felt that articles written by other scientists and researchers would carry more weight and be better received by farmers and those at the federal level when reporting to congressmen and requesting funding. Growers would be given free copies of these journals for a year, thereby exposing them to a range of current information and fostering better growing practices. The team would also encourage homemakers to use peanuts by sharing recipes and knowledge about nutrition and increased family health. Last but not least, the team meant to make better-quality seeds available to the growers.

EARLY ON, BARRY HAD WANTED to know who was involved in peanut disease research in the U.S. and overseas so that he could contact as many sources as possible to request pertinent information. One of Barry's letters was addressed to Tuskegee Institute, marking the beginning of the discussion of peanut diseases between the Tom Huston Peanut Company and Carver. On February 16, 1929, Carver wrote Barry that his letter to the Institute had been referred to him. In reply to Barry's question, Carver said:

... As far as I have been able to learn, and I have not followed up this part of it closely, but I should say that peanuts should run from eighty to ninety percent full plump, well matured kernels, true to the type of nut grown.

The discoloration, shriveling, wrinkleing, etc., may be due to any one or all of the following causes.

Bad selection of soil and its preparation.

(b) Seed not adapted to the soil or climate, inferior seed, etc.

(c) Diseases, the peanut often suffers from two very troublesome diseases.

First, [illegible] disease of the leaf (Cercospora personata) often partly or wholly defoliating the plant, causing the shriveling and wrinkleing of the nuts.

Second, a disease of the root, Neocosmospora, vasinfecta, it discolors both the nuts and the roots, in fact in some fields damages ninety per cent of the nuts, making discolorations, shrivels, etc.

(d) Immature plants would cause wrinkleing and shriveling as well as improper curing.

(e) Faulty polonation would also cause shriveling and wrinkleing.

Small inferior kernels not true to the type wanted should not be planted. Seed from an appreciable amount of diseased plants in the field should not be planted. And under no circumstances plant the seed from a diseased vine.

I am not sure whether I have answered your questions intelligently or not. If I am not clear let me know, and I shall try to make it so.

Yours very truly

G. W. Carver

Department of Agricultural Research and Experimental Station[77]

As early as 1914, Carver had begun preparing exhibits of food products, as well as medicinal vegetables, fruits, and herbs that could be grown in

Alabama by the average farmer. He assembled a large exhibit for the Macon County Fair which included jars of canned, dried, pickled, and preserved fruits and vegetables. He had taken his exhibit to many states, East and West, and had received enthusiastic responses. Carver had shared his message with congressmen in Washington, D.C. His 1916 Bulletin No. 31 on the peanut was reprinted in June 1925, with the addition of "105 Ways of Preparation." Therefore it was no surprise that Carver offered Huston suggestions focusing on the importance of educating the public when new ideas for the use of any new food products were being introduced to the marketplace. This is the basis of the partnership between Huston and Carver, and the very essence of true Extension community outreach, still true today.

In a letter to Huston dated September 23, 1929, Carver offers his advice:

> ... The public has to be educated on use of any new food product, to make its use universal and function in a large way. . . . In the course of time, I believe you will issue little educational leaflets, . . . making them attractive for the classroom, cooking classes, house wives, and farmers, which to my mind will help the whole peanut industry, even internationally. . . . "The Empty Dinner Pail" is one of our greatest national problems. Your great commercial and educational institution will make a great contribution to this and by giving and demonstrating to the world how easy it is to get a cheap, wholesome, nutritious appetizing, well balanced food stuff from the peanut.[78]

Since the beginning of their agreement to work together, Huston and Carver had exchanged many letters and had visited each other's workplace. They had developed a deep relationship based on an intense mutual respect, both personal and professional. Each had come to a clear understanding of the needs and goals of the other, and both realized that to be successful hours and days of work would be required. Carver also had interacted with Barry and Porter, and they too had developed respect for each other and an understanding of their different roles.

THE NEWLY FORMED TEAM HIT the ground running. Barry would present the directives of Huston from the Tom Huston Peanut Company.

The team decided on a model for working together in which the three men would share equally in input and correspondence. Barry and Porter wanted to learn as much as possible about the peanut and the needs for growing the crop, and Carver wanted to learn more about the Tom Huston Company's expanded plant operations. The three realized that they needed to be in a research mode, which would permit them to collect and document information. Also, as an education and public relations effort, they agreed that Porter would visit the peanut growers' fields to collect information that would help the company understand problems that would affect the quality and quantity of the peanut supply for the Tom Huston Company, specifically, as well as the industry. While visiting the growers, Porter would get to know them and begin to build trust and a collaborative relationship. If there were problems, the folks from the Tom Huston Peanut Company would do all they could to help solve them.

All three men realized that there was a problem with diseases affecting the peanut crops, but no one at higher levels of agriculture seemed to notice or be interested. This critical fact had become part of their mission: to learn more about these diseases.

In a letter from Carver to Barry, March 12, 1930, Carver answered Barry's question about previous consultations for soil analysis, peanut plants without nodules, and the need to inoculate the soil:

> . . . I wish to say that no soil requiring inoculation for peanuts has been brought to my attention. In fact, I have examined no plants that did not have nodules. Any plants having an abundance of nodules need no inoculation. If the plants do not form nodules one of two things may be necessary: first, inoculation; second, too much nitrogen has been used (which is not likely). Legumes should get their nitrogen from the air through these little germs that fasten themselves upon the roots and collect free nitrogen from the air. And as I stated before, that if the nitrogen is in the soil already, the nodule will not form, even though the nodule producing bacteria are there.
>
> Very truly yours
> G. W. Carver, Director
> Agricultural Research and Experiment Station[79]

THE FOLLOWING SERIES OF letters, beginning in August 1930 and continuing through 1932, shows the depth of cooperation between the Tom Huston folks and Carver and is a tribute to the seriousness of the problem which they had agreed to investigate. It is hoped that the reader will develop some sense of the depth of the issues, that this in a sense was pioneer work, and the ability and dedication of the three men to work together during this period of segregation is simply phenomenal. Some of the letters are long but are included in their entirety because they indicate the critical importance of the information being uncovered and have such a huge impact on the successful outcome of the project. The reader is urged to remember that the Tom Huston Company, a business enterprise and a buyer of peanuts, was not a supplier, yet the company chose to play a larger role in helping growers to produce a better product. This issue had then become the mission of the Tom Huston Company: that all involved in the industry must come to appreciate the significant impact that peanut diseases were having on the quality and amount of the product in the field at that time.

For several months during the growing season, Porter had been collecting samples of diseased plants and soils from the fields when he visited peanut growers and had been forwarding them to Carver. As they continued to collect samples and experiment with growing the plants, they were beginning to see some results that could be fed into their database. Barry wrote to ask Carver if he could come over to Tuskegee for a face-to-face meeting.

Dear Dr. Carver:-

If convenient to you I would like to run by and see you next Thursday morning. We have this season been experimenting with the culture of the Big Va. Bunch peanut in Ga. Have succeeded in making the vines put on a large number of peanuts and most of them have kernels in them but the kernels rot in the shell. When I come down I will bring Mr. Grady Porter, our field man, and some of the Va. Bunch vines with the nuts on them. They will interest you and also you might be able to tell us what causes the rot and how to overcome it. Please advise and thanks.

Cordially yours,

Tom Huston Peanut Company.,
Bob Barry, Mgr.,
Shelling Dept.[80]

In Carver's handwriting at the bottom right of the letter are the words, "Neocosmospora Vusinfecta.(*sic*)"

Carver wrote to Porter that, on the recent samples Porter had brought over, he had found a "reddish" disease on peanuts which had been found already on cotton. This was a new finding for the peanut, and he would work on a control method.[81]

To protect the integrity of their research, Barry also sent both inquiries and duplicate sample specimens to professional researchers, both in Washington, D.C., and to Agricultural Extension offices in the Southeastern states. The following is an example of the letters, this one sent to Mr. J. H. Beattie, assistant horticulturist at the U.S. Dept. of Agriculture in Washington on August 1, 1930:

Dear Dr. Beattie: -
Our field man, Mr. Grady Porter, is expressing you from Ft. Gaines, Ga. a bunch of Va. Bunch peanuts raised in the Southeast this season.

You will notice that we have succeeded in putting a large number of peanuts on the vine and that most of them have kernels in them but that a very high % of the kernels have rotted. Some of the kernels reach full size and then rot and shrivel down.

Please do all you can to tell us what the trouble is and how to overcome it. These peanuts were planted in 10 different tracts over the peanut belts of Ga., Fla. and Ala. and on many different kinds of soil.

1000# of ground limestone was drilled in or broadcast at planting time, to each acre. All plots were fertilized with different kinds of formulae. The lime should have been put down several months ahead of planting time.

Every tract of peanuts, under all the varying conditions have developed this rot.

We will greatly appreciate an extended effort on your part to tell us all you can about it.

Cordially yours,
TOM HUSTON PEANUT CO.,
Bob Barry, Mgr.,
Shelling Dept.[82]

Barry informed Carver on August 15, 1930, of the responses he had received on the subject

In regard to the trouble with Virginia peanuts in the Southeast, please be advised that I have heard from a good many different parties on the subject. Several of them think that it is a fungus disease Rhizoctonia. Please advise if you see any indication of it.

Some say it is a deficiency trouble on account of not using gypsum but we used gypsum on some of them without seeing any difference.

I understood you to say that you were going to make some tests with the bunches we left with you and are wondering if you have yet found time to do it.

As things develop we will gladly keep you posted.[83]

Barry followed up with a response to Carver, following receipt of Carver's letter of August 16:

... It is very gratifying to know that you are going into the Virginia peanut trouble so deeply. We feel that you are more competent to work this out than anybody we know.

It would be a capital idea for you to visit one of the infected fields and I see no reason why it cannot be satisfactorily arranged. This week I am handling the confection plant in the absence of the man in charge. Next Saturday I expect to go on my vacation and will be gone ten days. However, our Mr. Porter, whom you know should be able to take you to one of these fields, without any expense to you at all, and bring you back the same day. He will be here Thursday and I will try to arrange the matter and advise you further.[84]

On August 30, 1930, Carver received a letter from E. H. Patterson, Shelling Department, with an attached report that Carver had requested

THE PLAN AND THE ULTIMATE STRATEGY

upon his recent visit to the Tom Huston Peanut Company. It was from Arthur Frank, Pathologist, Brown Company, Belle Glade, Fla., and was entitled "Report on Virginia Peanut Disease." This would be an important document because, as the investigations continued, it became obvious that not only was there a paucity of information about peanut diseases, but that very few institutions were conducting research on the diseases of peanuts. [85]

Carver wrote to Grady Porter on September 1, 1930, informing him of the results of his examination of the plants that he (Porter) had recently brought over to Tuskegee:

My dear Mr. Porter:

You will be interested to know that I was able to find on one of the plants the perfect form of the "reddish" disease.

It belongs to the great family of fungi known as Hypocreaceae, of which there are a great many forms.

There are only three that need to concern us here in the South at present; viz, Neocosmospora, Nectria, and Claviceps, in the order named.

One of the most destructive diseases of cotton is due to Neocosmospora vasinfecta, sometimes called Fusarium vasinfectum, cotton wilt is due to this disease.

Several years ago I discovered a little of it on Spanish peanuts, affecting the roots, pods, and even the seed. This is the only time I have observed this disease until you and Mr. Barry brought it in a few weeks ago.

These peanuts of mine followed cotton and peas, both of which wilted badly.

There are quite a number of wilt diseases of plants, some appearing on the tomato, okra, ginseng, flax, etc. The mature stage of some has never been found, so therefore, it is impossible to tell to just what group they belong.

Control Methods For Neocosmospora:

Much work has been done to control this cotton wilt. All have proven more or less a failure. The most successful and the most hopeful [word "helpful" crossed out] remedy seems to be that of selecting types the most resistant to the wilt disease. Indeed they have now varieties of cotton and cow peas that resist the wilt almost perfectly. This is done mainly by the selection of resistant plants in badly infected fields, just as you suggested for the peanut.

This in connection with your proposed greenhouse experimental work will, I believe give you important information as to its control. I am sure it can be controlled in time.

The problem is new for peanuts and right now is the most favorable time to work out control measures most affectively.

I find also a new trouble which should receive attention. A disease caused by a fungus known as Diplodia. I was astonished to find it on the roots, stems, and hulls of the peanut, also on the roots and stems of two members of the wild Senna family (Cassia Marylandica and Cassia Tora) both species growing in the field with the peanuts. At the present time, I am not able to say whether it is a true parasite, saprophyte or facultative. With your assistance I hope to make an exhaustive study of it and settle those important questions.

I shall consider it a great privilege to cooperate with you and Mr. Barry in any way I can in your efforts to suppress these diseases which threaten one of the South's great money crops.

If I can help you call upon me at any time. There is also a Sclerotic trouble that I have not had the time to investigate.

Yours very truly

G. W. Carver, Director

Agricultural Research and Experiment Station[86]

The preceding letter, although long, is included in its entirety because it documents not only the disease affecting the sample peanuts, but also Carver's history of earlier identification, method of dealing with the disease, and additional diseases that he has found that must be recognized and treated. It is a wonderful portrayal of scientific genius expressed in simple terms.

Barry and Porter continued to collect specimens and bring them over to Carver. Both men visited on September 12, 1930, bringing both soil and plant samples Barry had collected while on a recent trip to Virginia. [87] The following week, Carver visited the Tom Huston Company to discuss continuing plans. Walter A. Richards, vice president, wrote to Carver to apologize for not having been able to meet him while he was in the plant. He wanted Carver to know that "I have been in close touch with the excellent work you are doing on the peanut diseases and I want you to know we deeply appreciate your cooperation."[88]

In a very interesting letter which demonstrates the sensitivity to the race situation still existing in the South, especially as applied to his relationship with Carver, Barry wrote and explained that he had recently received a request from Charles J. Brockway asking for his help in obtaining items for a peanut exhibit for a fair. He had replied that he had so much that might be useful that he recommended Brockway come over to Columbus and pick from the vast number of potential items. After mailing the letter, Barry said that it occurred to him that, "Mr. Brockway might be a colored man and feel a hesitancy in accepting my invitation." He asked Carver to call the man and explain to him that, "I do not care what color his skin is as long as he is doing something constructive along peanut lines. My office is open to anybody who is doing that." He also told Carver that he had written the man again, but still had no reply, and he thought that the race issue might be the reason.[89]

In a second letter to Carver, dated September 16, 1930, Barry shared additional concerns. This letter is important because it provides an example of the challenges of attracting the interest of government officials. Since every aspect of this new plan required a design from scratch, it was important to remember that this team was pioneering the effort from the ground up. There were no guidelines from previous studies, or efforts for peanuts, to go by. And perhaps even more important to understand is that those involved were outside the "magic circle" of the powerful land grant institutions that had direct links to the officials at the federal level, including the Department of Agriculture through its Experiment Stations, Cooperative Extension, and County Agents.

Dear Dr. Carver:

My mind has been going around in circles trying to decide what I think is the best thing to do about these peanut diseases so far as the agricultural experts of the country are concerned. Whatever we do will be approved by you first so I would like to tell you what's on my mind at present.

Possibly some high official in the Department of Agriculture in Washington could be startled into an appreciation of the seriousness of the situation. He could call a meeting of the agricultural powers of the Southeastern States and learn all the details of your discoveries. It might be the rest of them would boo at the situation because somebody else found it out. Then too people in political jobs are not looking for hard work as a rule. If they did attempt to do something the chances are they would scare the farmer to death and cause him to reduce his peanut acreage unreasonably. As Grady Porter puts it, it would be like running a bear out in front of him without giving him anything to shoot him with.

I am inclined to believe that the following is the best method to pursue. You have found out what the trouble is. The next thing is to find some way to overcome it. We might be able to do this in the greenhouse this Winter. If so, we can get everybody busy next Summer after the crops have been planted and advise them how to save them.

I would like to have your candid and frank opinion of it, telling me how I am wrong and why if you think so.

Hope to see you again in the very near future.

It is interesting that a day earlier Carver had written to his long-time friend, Dr. M. L. Ross, and shared with him the following:

My beloved friend, Dr. Ross:-
. . . All last week I was called upon to inspect farms of peanuts in Ga. Ala. and Fla. A very serious disease has appeared among them.

They have had it before the leading experts in Washington D.C. and many Exp. Stations, they knew nothing about it. I happened to know what it was from experience. I have to make another trip tomorrow to see these infected fields. There is much microscopic work to be done. . . .

Admiringly yours,

G. W. Carver [Entire letter handwritten][90]

Ross was an old friend, a physician from Topeka, Kansas, with whom Carver corresponded regularly. At Carver's encouragement, Ross was now involved in medical research on animals.[91]

IN FURTHER INDICATION OF how much time Barry had spent working out the details for implementation of the plan, he wrote Carver three different letters dated September 18, 1930. The first advised Carver:

> Enclosed you will find a form which I have made out which, when it is filled out, will give us a record of the information we need about peanut diseases. I have filled out what I could about Neocosmosfora Vasinfecta and would like to have you change it or complete it as is necessary. Each of the other sheets are headed with the different kinds of disease and could be filled out in the same manner.

Page 1 of form that Barry sent to Carver.

You are so much more competent to do this than we are that I am sending it on to you. If we ask you to do too much please tell us so because I haven't seen any signs of that yet.

If you can find time to complete these forms I will be glad to make a copy of them and send them on to you.

Mr. Porter left for Virginia this morning and I told him not to spare the dollars to call you on the telephone any time he thought you would want him to.[92]

The second letter apprised Carver that Barry had sent copies of two books that the Tom Huston Peanut Company had published: one on the culture and marketing of peanuts and another on grading. Barry sent extra copies for him to share.[93]

In the third letter, Barry advised Carver that a local farmer told him that "his tomatoes, snapbeans, and spinach were practically ruined by the white mould (sic) which you have discovered on peanuts."[94]

In a letter dated September 19, 1930, Carver responded to Barry's request to contact Brockway, telling him of their conversation and adding a surprising new issue for continued cooperation:

... Mr. Chas. Brockway is a white man, broad and generous, very intelligent, and a graduate of Auburn. I am sure you will like him. I just had a long conference with him yesterday. I am confident that he will call upon you before long. I am doing what I can to help him with his peanut exhibit. We hope to break down the "taboo" which now exists upon peanut fed pork claiming that it is inferior etc., etc. A ban has been placed upon it here in Alabama. I saw last week in the Montgomery Advertiser that Tuskegee Institute had refused to purchase it along with other institutions, etc.

I am now trying to locate some peanut fed pork, bacon, etc. I want to make a critical study of it to see just how much of it is true and if such a trouble cannot be corrected as easily as the soft pork made from feeding acorns. I believe it can. It means much now in dollar and cents to a great and growing Southern money crop.

Your letter assures me further that my people who are interested in growing peanuts can come to your office without fear of it being impressed upon them that they were not wanted. Of course, I have been knowing this for sometime. Had this not been true, it would have been absolutely impossible for me to have cooperated with you and Mr. Porter in working out these peanut diseases.

I am exceeding grateful to you both for such a rare opportunity. When we get through, I believe it is going to be one of the biggest things in the way of a contribution that has come to southern peanut growers for sometime.

The circle in which your mind is revolving is correct. We need to do some more investigating and find more things to definitely clinch it and unquestionably prove that the peanut is susceptible to the same wilt as cotton, tomatoes, etc. We only need a little more evidence.

You brought some splendid things from Virginia, invaluable in working these diseases out.

I am expecting Mr. Porter to bring back an equally good report, with specimens from another section of Virginia. He said if he got sorely puzzled he would call me up while there.

I believe with you, that we ought not to bother any more Micologists with it. We are in much better position to work it out than they are.

Under no circumstances should the farmer be excited, but when we get the results from your experimental work this winter, possibly a little sheet might be gotten out to supplement your splendid bulletins which are so full of just what the farmers need plainly put.

I believe it would be wise to talk to as many peanut growers as possible, asking them if their yield was satisfactory, if not why. Save plenty of the infected plants to show them. Then before planting time in the spring, we will be able to tell them just what to do.

I have already told Mr. Porter in talking with him the other day, to tell the farmer who has so much of this "Witches-broom" in his field not to save seed from this field, and not to put the same land in peanuts next year. I would like to get this witches-broom on cotton. Mr. Porter tells me that he has seen it.

You are absolutely correct in your way of thinking. I shall be glad to get anything bearing upon these diseases that you find on plants of any kind. I shall also be glad to have you come over at your earliest convenience, and we will talk the whole matter over. You have the idea well in mind.

I am very happy to know that this work in being done through the Tom

Huston Company. We must begin with the farmer before the crop is planted, and of course afterwards.[95]

The conversations continued as Barry asked Carver, in a letter dated September 19, 1930, if he understood Carver correctly as saying he thought sulfur would do some good. Barry wrote, ". . . It has occurred to me that a fertilizer with sulphate of ammonia and sulphate of potash, along with the phosphoric acid which is made from sulphuric (sic) acid and phosphate rock, might be a better proposition than the fertilizers customarily used for peanuts . . ."[96] He asked Carver for his thoughts.

Barry followed up with the previously raised issue of peanut-fed meat. He told Carver that he had written the manager of the Swift packing house in Moultrie, Georgia, asking for samples of meat, and he apprised Carver of the fact that Swift made a specialty of a delicious peanut ham. He further suggested that Carver write Swift directly and explain his needs, because Barry felt certain that Swift would supply him.[97]

PORTER NOTIFIED CARVER THAT when he arrived in Chowan County, Virginia, he found that there had been no rain in over two months, and, as a result, everything was badly wilted, and many plants had died. Nevertheless, he was sending samples which would find very interesting. Porter indicated that he found signs of what he thought were Cosmosphora, Diplodia, and Schletoria; and he hoped that Carver would have better luck with positive identification than he had been able to. He told Carver that when Carver had had time to receive and examine the specimens, he would call for suggestions to help with this situation. He added, "P. S. An application of from four hundred to six hundred pounds of top dressing was applied to the fields from which these specimens were taken at blooming time. I haven't as yet found a field where they did not use this top dressing."[98]

Early in 1930 and continuing during this same time period, the team had been discussing the value of some research of their own to be conducted in a greenhouse over the winter. Barry stated that ". . . Neither Mr. Porter nor myself are scientists. We simply try to make practical application of what scientists tell us. Hence your frank criticism of anything we do will be just what we want."[99] The team agreed to wait for responses to their inquiries before finalizing the plan. One of the few researchers to respond to Barry's request for information was Dr. Arthur Frank, Pathologist, Brown Company, Belle Glade, Florida. As previously mentioned, Frank also sent a copy of his report on diseases of the Virginia peanut.[100] In a letter to Carver, Barry explained that after talking to others he did not feel that a greenhouse experiment would yield results, since, in actual use, efforts would be applied over a large territory with greatly varying field conditions. Also, in a greenhouse, it would be difficult to get the fungus to attack the peanuts at a desired stage. After further discussion, the team, based on Porter's recommendation, abandoned the greenhouse plan that would have cost money and additional work and would not have accurately represented actual field conditions. The change would allow time for plans for the next spring to be worked out carefully for field conditions and to go after the diseases in the summer in a practical way. Barry assured Carver that he [Carver] would be the deciding factor in what should be done. He attached two reports published by the Tom Huston Company: "Peanut Grades of Small White Spanish Farmers Stock" and "Various Analyses on Commercial Peanut Hulls."[101] [See Appendix A]

One expert who dispensed recommendations that were followed by many peanut growers was Dr. J. H. Beattie, an assistant horticulturist with the U.S. Department of Agriculture. In August 1930, Barry had written Beattie advising him that Porter was sending some specimens of Virginia Bunch peanuts grown in Fort Gaines, Georgia, during this season, and asked for his advice. Beattie responded that "the disease was not the cause of the failure to mature of the Virginia-type peanut but was the effect of the problem."

Neither Barry nor Porter were comfortable with this response.

PORTER CONTINUED TO VISIT peanut growers in southeastern states and to collect specimens of plants showing effects of disease. During these visits, he found plants other than peanuts being affected by similar symptoms. Barry reminded Carver of what he, himself, had learned earlier from a local farmer that, "his tomatoes, snap beans, and spinach were practically ruined by the white mould (sic) which you have discovered on peanuts."[102]

A new issue was discovered by Barry and Porter during the latter part of 1930, that of leaving too much of the peanut crop unharvested. In a letter to Carver, Barry explained:

Mr. West at Ft. Gaines measured off 10 feet square in our prize thirty acres of Small Spanish and scratched out the peanuts which were left in the ground. There were two pounds in 100 square feet. This amounts to 870 pounds per acre. I have looked through the records as far as 1918 and find that no State in any of the Peanut Belt has ever produced 870 pounds to the acre, total, except that North Carolina did several different years. This is evident that our Southeastern soils are still producing good yields of peanuts but that the profit is left in the ground instead of going to the farmers pockets.

I am sending you the box of peanuts which Mr. West sent me. If we take off 25% for the weight of the sprouts, sand etc. it would still mean 652 pounds of peanuts to the acre left in the ground.

What could be more serious than this?[103]

The following day, Barry again wrote Carver, explaining that:

Mr. Richards thinks that we should have a number of different parties scratch up part of the peanuts left in the ground, this year, and weigh them so that we will have enough evidence to make the public sit up and take notice when we are ready to tell them something. He thinks that if each of you Mr. Porter and myself do that in one or two fields we would then be eye witnesses and then the information would be of much more value.

If you have no objections I will write to all of the experiment stations and ask them to mark off about 20 feet square and dig the peanuts up and weigh them. Will offer to pay the labor charge. Will not tell them anything about peanut diseases but simply say we are trying to determine how many peanuts are left in the ground after harvesting. Might also ask them to tell us their opinion about why they were left in the ground.[104]

In September, Barry wrote Carver that he was glad Carver liked the form Barry had devised to collect information on peanut diseases. He assured Carver that Porter had been told that Carver wanted to find the *Neocosmospora* on cotton so that he could be mycologically safe. Barry said he would try to locate specimens of the white mold on spinach, tomatoes, and beans though he feared it might be too late in the season. He admitted that he had been under the impression that *Neocosmospora* and *Fusarium* were the same disease, just showing up in different formations. Barry wanted to ensure that others were not similarly confused, so he suggested using two of the new forms, each annotated to clarify the matter. He asked that they set up a conference as soon as convenient, for the purpose of determining and documenting exactly what the team wanted to accomplish in the greenhouse.[105]

STILL COLLECTING SAMPLES IN North Carolina, Porter wrote Carver that he had sent a package with samples from Williamston that appeared to exhibit the same conditions as those from Chowan. Rainfall was still low, and Porter pointed out that Carver should notice a total absence of any peanuts or pins. He also told Carver that a large percentage of the cotton in all counties in the peanut-growing area was badly infected. The county Extension agent there told Porter that the problem was Anthracnose, but Porter told Carver that the roots seem to have the same infection "as our cotton." Porter said he was being very careful to distinguish between plants that are wilted due to disease and those wilted from lack of water.[106]

Barry sent Carver a clipping from the *Columbus Ledger* featuring an editorial discussing peanut-fed pork versus corn-fed pork. Opinions were quoted, and the statement is made that "somebody should work it out and settle the matter." Barry told Carver that he was tempted to inform the newspaper that Carver was already doing that type of work, but he wanted Carver's permission first. Barry closed, "It is good to hear you say that there are only a few things to find out now before we will have all the facts we want. I hope that we can get it all on paper so that it can easily be referred to in the future." [107] By this time, Barry had received responses from three overseas Extension programs, in Australia, India, and South Africa, discussing diseases they had found.[108] Barry evidently had a problem with the terms used in the correspondence from South

Africa, because he wrote Carver to thank him "for his letter of the 19th regarding the difference in the African and American language regarding peanut diseases. It will be well for us all to bear this in mind in figuring the proposition out."[109] Such global collaboration in regard to daunting crop diseases continues to the present day.

Barry notified Carver that he went out to a farm near Warm Springs, Georgia, and met a peanut grower who was digging and stacking his peanuts. They measured off an area twenty feet square and scratched out all the peanuts left in the ground, which amounted to only 1¼ ounces (just 8½ pounds to the acre). Barry said the peanuts were basically disease-free as far as he could tell with the naked eye. He said he was sending specimens of both the peanuts and vines with the peanuts attached.[110]

While still in the field collecting specimens, Porter notified Carver that he was sending yet more boxes of samples, this time from around Suffolk. He told Carver that the soil type around Suffolk, which Porter identified as "the Virginia peanut territory as a whole," was of a lighter type than the North Carolina section, which he felt had caused that particular area to be affected more by the drought. He also shared:

... I believe that you will be especially interested in the soy beans in this shipment. I am told by Mr. Batten that the Virginia College advises him that Anthrocnose causes all the trouble with the peanuts, and the cotton, and the soy beans. Mr. Batton says further that losses like this in cotton, soy beans and peanuts are not noticeable. This Mr. Batton that I speak of, is in charge of one of the state's experiment farms. This one being located at Holland Va. I don't agree with Mr. Batton and his advise from the college, and I wonder if you do....

To-morrow and next day I am going to try and find one or more [fields] of Small Spanish. Hoping that I will be able to find something that will be of interest to us.[111]

As the data-gathering efforts of the team begin to produce results, Barry wrote to Carver thanking him for his recent letters:

... It is gratifying to know that you feel we are getting somewhere.
You can rest assured that Mr. Porter will find what you want in Virginia if

it is up there. As soon as he gets back let's all get together and talk things over.

I hope that we are not over-burdening you. There are so many things that you can and will do that I am beginning to wish that you were either twins or triplets. I guess however it is too late to do anything about that.[112]

Realizing that the Alabama growers had been unresponsive to offers of assistance, Carver requested that Porter do some investigative work around the town of Enterprise, Alabama. Barry advised that on the day that they had eaten dinner in Tuskegee, he and Porter discussed the Runner situation, especially in Alabama, and that, as soon as Porter returned from Virginia he would go down into the Runner section to see the effects of the diseases on that variety.[113]

In the meantime, Barry received a response from Dr. R. F. Poole, a plant pathologist in the Department of Botany, at the North Carolina State College of Agriculture and Engineering (now North Carolina State University) in Raleigh, North Carolina. Barry wrote Carver, attaching a copy of the September 27, 1930, letter from Poole stating that bacterial wilt, the Fusarial wilt, and the Cercospora leaf spot were present on peanuts in that area. Poole explained that from his experience the wilts were different from the specimen Barry had sent to him "in that the organism enters the base of the stem and works up into the tissues, finally killing the plant. The infection may or may not interfere with the production of nuts until the plant is killed." Poole went on:

We also have the injury on the pods caused by the Corticum vagum fungus. The popular name for this is the Rhizoctonia disease. This same organism causes sore shin on tobacco, tomatoes and peppers in this State. We also have the trouble of obtaining full pods, such as occurred on the specimens that you sent me. This, of course, has been diagnosed by us as being physiological. That is, it is thought that no organism is involved in the condition whereby the plant fails to develop full pods. The farmers of this State without any scientific backing have learned that applications of gypsum to the plant is inductive to nut formation. As Dr. Mann has probably told you he finds that this really is

beneficial in some recent experiments conducted by himself. There is no question but what this is the important one with you, because the dying back of
the tips and the blackening of some of the nuts may easily be physiological in
which saprophytes play an important part. If the roots of the plant were badly
diseased we would necessarily have to work on an entirely different theory.[114]

AS THE NUMBER OF peanut diseases identified by Carver and others
increased, Barry sent Carver additional copies of the Data Collection Form
for Peanut Diseases, telling Carver that "We will have to fill them out in
your presence to be sure we are getting them right so I thought it would
be better for them to be in your file than in ours." [115] Six diseases were now
listed on the attached forms: *"Neocosmospora vasinfecta, Fusarium vasinfecta,
Sclerotia, Ozonium auricomum, Diplodia, and Witches Broom."*[116]

At this same time, Carver received a detailed letter from Mr. H. Mc-
Dowell, a manager with Swift & Company. McDowell acknowledged
that Alabama hog farmers were paid less for peanut-fed hogs than western
corn-fed hogs and that packers must sell peanut-fed hog products cheaper,
because the appearance of the product was undesirable: that is, it was soft,
oily, and harder to slice. The appearance and consequently the sales were
affected because housewives had an aversion to a shiny, oily-looking product. However, McDowell said, the meat had a fine flavor and "the southern
people" seem to prefer it. He felt that the flavor was due to the animals being
fed the peanut diet; therefore, the company was trying to capitalize on this
quality. Swift & Company had put on the market "a Peanut Brand Ham
and a Peanut Brand Picnic Shoulder, at full market price." Only 5 percent
of the product was being sold at market price. The balance were being sold
at a two-cent discount. McDowell said Swift & Company felt it would take
years before these products were accepted by the public at market price.

McDowell told Carver that Swift would be glad to furnish whatever
samples Carver desired. He attached, for Carver's information, a document
entitled "Peanut Pork: A New Food Delicacy," plus other information on
the subject, including two bulletins issued by USDA.[117]

THE YEAR WAS FAST coming to an end, and the team had collected vast amounts of information. More was coming in. The hours of planning and field work were beginning to pay off. Barry wrote to Carver that he had attended a called meeting of the Southeastern Peanut Association in September, and during the meeting had remarked that, "I had noticed a good many peanuts left in the ground this year and thought that everybody should look into it and see what the trouble was." A man in the audience spoke up and said he had noticed a disease a few years back and had sent specimens to Washington. Although he had received a full report with the diagnosis that the problem was due to some form of fungus, he was not given any information as to what to do about it. Barry told Carver:

> I got a motion passed whereby the Secretary of the Association will send a circular letter to every member of the Association and state that it has been reported that a good many peanuts are left in the ground after gathering. This letter will request them to make an investigation in their immediate section, without alarming the farmer, and make a report at the next call meeting. I believe this will get the right thinking matter in their minds without interfering with the work we want to do.[118]

Carver was by then busy preparing his exhibit for the Alabama State Fair in Montgomery that would run from October 20 through 24, 1930. He alerted Barry and Porter that he had found another link confirming their investigations to peanut diseases.

> . . . I found Neocosmospora vasinfecta on the roots of the cow pea. I went out into the pea field Saturday and pulled up quite a number of dead vines. Part of the roots were literally pink with it. This made me feel very happy as I had been looking for it on the pea for sometime.
>
> After our busy season is over, we will be ready to get all the information we have to get and dispose of it in what ever way we feel wise.
>
> I want to again express my appreciation to you and Mr. Porter for giving me this opportunity. I feel very happy over the results.[119]

Barry replied that he was glad that Carver had found the *Neocosmospora vasinfecta* on the roots of the cow pea. He said that he also now felt that they are all set to "take the situation by the throat as soon as we can get to it." He further stated that Mr. Brockway from Auburn was just in the Columbus office, and he gave him quite a bit of material for his peanut exhibit at the Fair in Montgomery.[120]

Still interested in channeling their waste materials into something of use, Barry wrote to Carver and expressed interest in shipping cases made from peanut hulls. He asked Carver for suggestions. He explained that "the waste of peanut hulls is an important factor in the value of peanuts from the farm. Many thousands of dollars are paid out every year to freight these hulls into shellers who can do nothing with them but burn them up. A profitable outlet for them should enable all peanut buyers to pay more for the farm product."[121]

Carver responded that this very good idea should be followed up. He supplied Barry with the names of two mills in the South that made wood pulp for paper. He told Barry that he had pulped peanut hulls in his laboratory and made crude blocks of paper and that he had gotten a good sort of "straw board" suitable for boxes. Carver thought the yield from pulp from peanut hulls would be much lower than the products then in use.[122]

IN NOVEMBER 1930, CARVER began a speaking tour through several states in the East. He spoke about the peanut and demonstrated his exhibit as often as he could. Before he left, he advised Barry that he had found Fusarium, Sclerotina, and Rhizoctonia on the pick-outs that Porter had given to him at the Fair in Montgomery. Barry replied that he was "glad that you told me that a farmer brought in some bunches of peanuts and young peanut plants that had Sclerotina on the roots and stems," but he was sorry that the farmer had lost most of his crop. He told Carver that he wouldn't be surprised if many more farmers were in the same situation.[123]

Although Carver had been publishing articles in *The Peanut Journal* for many years, it was becoming clear that enhanced methods were needed for sharing information and getting buy-in from peanut producers. This realization evolved into the idea of using a media blitz to flood agricultural journals with the information collected and learned since the team's plan was implemented. Journals were an excellent way to reach other researchers, interested stakeholders, and those with political and economic investments. In this case, a somewhat new crop with enormous potential to become a multimillion-dollar industry was threatened by poorly understood diseases. Funding was needed to study these diseases and to provide participating growers with assistance for the costs of best practices and control methods.

In a September 11, 1930, letter to *Peanut Journal* editor M. M. Osborn, Carver wrote:

> . . . I am especially pleased with Prof. John Gaub's article on "Why is not more Peanut Butter Used?" To my mind he has struck the very weakest link in the promotion of the consumption of peanuts.
>
> Peanuts as a confection has a wonderful sale and continue to grow in popularity; not simply because they are good but because the purchaser knows just what to do with them. But when it comes to using it as a vegetable, or seasoning, shortening, and enriching many other the foods in palatability, high protein content at low cost, they know practically nothing about.
>
> One demonstrator in every community like Prof. Gaub would in a comparatively short time have the peanut an essential part of the daily menu, reducing in a most sensible and logical way the high cost of living which is especially important this year.
>
> Housewives all over the country will not only welcome nut [but] grow enthusiastic over these demonstrations.
>
> Your proposed forum is the ideal thing to follow such demonstrations, as they will suggest many variations as well as new uses.
>
> If all of us work together to push this ideal advertising method, the peanut will soon be serving the people as its almost perfect composition and other good qualities warrant[124]

In a letter to Carver dated November 29, 1930, Barry wrote, "Sometime when you are not rushed I would like to have you tell me what a peanut is. Occasionally I am called on to make a short talk on peanuts by parties who are not interested in any particular phase of the industry. A talk of that kind would interest them. Is this asking too much?" [125] Carver evidently needed more information about what Barry wanted to learn from him, so Barry followed up with another letter:

> Let me see if I can explain what I had in mind about a little talk on peanuts. First I would like to tell what a peanut is agriculturally. I had in mind comparing it with humanity to make it more comprehensive. Thought of starting something like this: "Like I am a human being a peanut is a plant. Like I am of the Anglo-Saxon race, a peanut is a Legume. It is not a nut at all but belongs to the same plant classification as beans, peas, clover, alfalfa, etc. Like I am of the American race, a peanut is _____ (branch of legume group that has pea-shaped flowers). Etc" bringing it down to the finest division possible.
>
> Then I would like to take it up sexually and classify it and compare it with other plants that propagate in a different way.
>
> Would like to take it up chemically and say what percent of each ingredient it contains, and what function each performs if possible.
>
> Could ad[d] to this the importance of the peanut compared with other agricultural products, the production by Nations and state, etc.
>
> Would then have something that would fit any kind of audience. The part which didn't fit could be left out on any certain occasion.
>
> Will appreciate it if you will do some thinking along these lines, at your leisure, if you ever have any, and tell me what you think of it. [126]

AN INQUIRY CAME TO Barry from Dr. John Duggar, in the Department of Farm Management at Alabama Polytechnic Institute (now Auburn University), asking about brightening peanut hulls with sulfur fumes or other chemicals. Barry responded that he had never had any experience along this line, and that he was forwarding a copy of Duggar's letter to Carver, saying that "If anybody can answer your question satisfactorily he can." [127] Carver wrote Barry and thanked him for the copy of the letter to Duggar and for his generous reference. He told Barry that he would "be pleased to give Mr. Duggar this information in detail if he writes me." Carver then explained to Barry that:

I will say that considerable work has been done along this line, various bleaching agents have been tried out following out the same and similar methods
used by the California nut growers, but so far it has not been as satisfactory for
either pecan or peanuts as for walnuts, almonds, fi[l]berts, etc, *etc.* Sulphur
fumes and other chemical bleaching agents will do the work for a while, but
there are two main objections:

1st. The bleach for peanuts and pecans has not proven stable. In a few months
they revert back to a color less desirable than before they were bleached.

2nd. So far, no one has been able to get a uniform product. The bleach
seems to emphasize any deep seated spots or discolorations of the shell.[128]

AS THE TEAM BEGAN the New Year, Barry wrote Carver that he had just
completed the write-up of the Small Spanish test plots which Carver saw
at Fort Gaines, Georgia, and would mail him a copy. He assured Carver
that he would enjoy reading it. He also said that the Virginia tracts were
not on paper yet, but he would send the information as soon as he can.[129]
Shortly thereafter, Huston Company vice president Walter Richards wrote
Carver that:

I have just read my copy of the report on our experimental work by Mr. Barry and
Mr. Porter, in which they express appreciation of your great help, particularly
on the plant diseases.

I, of course, have been familiar with your work in this connection, but I want to
say again that we thank you most sincerely for your cooperation in this work.[130]

Of course, Carver responded to Richards, graciously thanking him for
his letter and saying:

. . . I am greatly indebted to Mr. Barry and Mr. Porter for their invaluable help
which was given without stint. Indeed they often went out of their way to get
such material as I wished to work with. It is a great pleasure for me to work
with these gentlemen, and I consider it a privilege to render such assistance
to an organization that is doing so much for southern agriculture especially.

... I am planning to cooperate more fully with Mr. Barry and Mr. Porter this year, beginning with the planting season.

I am still hoping that you will "break that trace" you spoke of and get over to see me, and take a little rest, as I know you need it . . .[131]

Barry wrote Carver:

I am getting all of my data together preparatory to making a report on Virginia peanuts, in the Southeast, for the 1930 growing season.

In looking over my file I find that you wrote the Iowa State College in September of 1930 about the peanut diseases. I do not find anything in the file which shows what they had to say about it and if you heard from them I would like to have a copy of the letter.

I want to get all of these reports out before calling on you if possible because I feel that all of us will then be better equipped to determine what to do to follow it up. Don't you think this is wise?[132]

Barry included a draft copy of his report on the Small Spanish for the season of 1930 grown on test plots in Fort Gaines, Georgia. This was perhaps the crux of the entire story, because it represented over a year of careful planning and action, and it placed in context the magnitude of the team's achievement. It identified the problem, what was done to prove it, and what should be done to rectify it. It was the first such research information available with such a scope, and it was achieved by two most unlikely entities. In the following excerpt from page 2, beginning with paragraph 4, Barry summarized the effort:

Five peanut diseases developed, not only in these tracts, but all over the peanut belt where they had late rains. These diseases have apparently been heretofore unknown to the Peanut Industry although there is now much evidence to show that they have existed ever since peanuts were first planted. Nobody has heretofore had enough interest to work it out, but we will. As you will see the yield of peanuts was governed by whether the conditions were more or less favorable to the diseases. This eliminated any chance to gain fertilizer information. But the knowledge gained about the diseases was of much more value. Especially as it affected the whole belt, has been taking its toll for nobody knows how long, is practically unknown to others and nobody is doing anything about it. We also proved by a practical demonstration that the methods outlined in our Culture Book will work and that very few farmers are getting half as many peanuts per acre as they should and could get.

We learned somewhat early in the season that peanut diseases were at work, although we did not know then what it was all about. We quickly pressed Dr. Carver of Tuskegee into service which was just what he wanted us to do and he worked with us continually throughout the season. We took him no end of specimens from all over the S. E. Peanut belt and got some from other belts of the United States. He isolated the 5 following diseases. Schleratina Diplodia, Neocosmospora Vasinfecta, Ozonium Auriconum and Witches Broom. The Schleratonia was especially rampant in Small Spanish varieties all over the belt where late rains had set in. Our tracts were alive with it. We had some Diplodia, a little ozonium auriconum and just a slight trace of Neocosmospora vasinfecta (sometimes called Fusarium Vasinfecta). Witches Broom did not appear in these tracts but elsewhere. We made many trips to see Dr. Carver and he made many patient studies with us under the microscope. He visited these fields and others. Other specialists along these lines also visited the fields.

All of these are fungus diseases and thrive best under moist conditions. They seem to be more apt to appear late in the life of a peanut than early. With a wet late season the diseases are favored for extreme destruction. We had this wet late season. Many peanut stems rotted off and left the peanut in the ground. These decayed there so badly that hogs would not eat them. Many other mature kernels became damaged to such an extent that the grade of the gathered peanuts was poor. The peanuts went through a wet curing season and some of these diseases carried on even in the stacks. You could shake a stack and an unusual amount of peanuts would drop out on the ground. We measured off 10 feet square in one of our fields, dug up the peanuts and weighed them. It amounted to 982# to the acre, almost as much as the yield we finally succeeded in retaining. We also tried this out in other fields in the peanut belt both in Ga. and Va. and found similar losses. In one peanut tract which was new ground we found practically nothing left in the ground. This

bears out the fact that the diseases come down from year to year from cultivated plants, most likely cotton or peas. We wrote to every Govt. employee
that should be interested and asked them to dig out a few small plots and
see what was left in the ground. We did not tell them what we knew because
we must not alarm anybody along this line until we can tell them what to do
about it. The peanut acreage would be reduced too much as a result. Simply
told them that we had noticed many left in the ground and to check us on it
in their locality and advise what they thought was the trouble. Not one did
anything and possibly never will.[133]

At the bottom of page 3, Barry stated, "Dr. Carver will be tickled to
death to work with us and there is nobody in the world that can do as much
along these lines. The harmony and co-operation that has existed between
Dr. Carver and Grady and myself has been a treat and an inspiration. It
will continue to be."

In an attached handwritten note, Barry asked Carver to carefully review
the report and let him know . . . "If I have slipped up anywhere in the report
and advise me."[134]

Several months earlier, Barry had made a similar comment about Carver
to Mr. W. P. Cutter, of the Baker Library at Harvard University:

Dr. Geo. W. Carver of the Tuskegee Institute at Tuskegee, Alabama is the fore-
most scientist of the World on peanut progress. He would be tickled to death
to work with you along the lines you are thinking and can give you a wealth of
information. Suggest that you write him.[135]

TWO DAYS AFTER CARVER received the copy of the report, Barry wrote
to let him know that he had not shared the draft report with anyone else
except Mr. H. P. Vannah of the Brown Company in the Florida Everglades.
Barry asked for Carver's advice as to whether the report should go to others
at the time. He also asked Carver to . . . "feel perfectly free to criticize any
and everything in it because it is my desire to have it right regardless of
everything else." Barry continued:

. . . Am glad to be able to tell you that I am getting along fine with my preparatory data for the tests on Virginia peanuts in the Southeast. I have been
somewhat surprised to find out how much information we did have and I am
taking particular pains to get it all together. . . . I believe that I will be able to
give it to you sometime this week and want you to pass judgement on it before
it goes to anybody else, including Tom. You see I want to get it right before he
sees it.[136]

Grady Porter was still in the field evaluating plants and collecting
specimens. He sent Carver a handwritten letter from Fort Gaines, Georgia,
updating him and explaining that the weather has impeded much of his
recent work, but assuring him that:

I have tried to keep on with our work with this idea in view (and I hope that
you agree) that since we know what is wrong with Virginia (Neocosmospora)
we also know that sclerotina is the Spanish worst enemy. I am trying now to
find what it is, (if anything) with runners.

I think if we can locate this we can try for them all, what do you think. I
am especially interested in the runners from what we shellers call concealed
damage. You know some years the farmers think they have good nuts, but after
they are shelled they have sour hearts. I believe this is a disease and am sure
if I can find it you can identify it, then we can work on it next year and maybe
by this method kill more than one bird with one stone . . .[137]

Barry meanwhile had received a letter from the Bogalusa Paper Company, dated January 8, 1931, containing a sample of paper made from "one
cook" of the peanut hulls sent from the Tom Huston Company. The samples
were dark gray, thick, rough rectangles similar to thick sandpaper. The
writer concluded that the results were not promising, suggested a different
processing method, and provided a referral to another company that was
using the suggested method.[138]

Later in January, Barry wrote to Carver that, like Carver, he did not think
much of the paper from peanut hulls from the Bogalusa Paper Company.
He also stated that he was trying to work with other companies to get them

to try the experiment with different processes. He told Carver, ". . . If we can say that all of our stationery and shipping boxes are made out of peanut hulls it will have both a distinct advertising value and will also encourage the farmers to know that somebody is trying to make their hulls an asset."[139]

Another critical part of the plan was the report of the peanut diseases that Carver had been developing and that was nearing completion. He notified Barry:

> Enclosed find my preliminary report, written in skeleton form somewhat, as we expect to investigate very thoroughly some of these minor diseases.
>
> Please feel perfectly free to use what you want, and hold the other in obeyance for further observation.
>
> You and Mr. Porter may want to add something to it that will make it serve the farmer much better than the way I have put it[140]

Carver attached a draft report entitled "How the Farmer Can Improve the Quantity and Quality of His Peanuts." It contained seven directives:

Plant only clean plump seed.
Plant only in a clean well prepared seed bed.
Use the proper quantity and quality of fertilizers.
Plant at least 75 pounds (in the hull) to the acre.
Thorough, frequent, shallow, and clean cultivation is necessary. This can be easily done with a weeder if used early. Hoeing should not be done as it invariably decreases the yield of nuts.
When your peanuts are ripe dig at once.
Stack carefully in small stacks by hand with nuts toward the pole.

The following three pages of Carver's draft report are included in their entirety because the contents represent the previous several months activities of field work and data collection and document Carver's contribution to the Tom Huston Company's plan. It was also the first of this kind of information specifically written in appropriate language to be shared with the farmers.

SOME PEANUT DISEASES

Early in July 1930, Mr. Bob Barry and Mr. Grady Porter, of the Tom Huston Peanut Company, Columbus Georgia, brought to my attention some troubles which were seriously affecting the hay and greatly reducing the quantity and quality of the nuts. Wherever they investigated, they found this trouble extending with greater or less severity where peanuts were grown in any considerable quantity in Georgia, Alabama, and Florida, also Virginia and North Carolina.

Microscopic examination of diseased plants revealed several specific troubles known commonly as wilt diseases. Technically as follows:

Neocosmospora Vasinfecta (Cotton Wilt)

This disease was easily identified as we had no trouble in finding the perfect form of the fungus which occurs on the outside of the peanut hull in red patches. It frequently occurs on the nut itself within the hull.

How it Effects the Plant

As far as we are able to find out at the present time, the peanut is attacked by the fungus the same as cotton causing it to wilt and die in various stages of its development. The blossom end of the nut seems to be attacked first, as it begins to turn dark brown, in fact begins to rot, proceeds upward until the whole pod is affected. The nut often becomes soft and decays.

FUSARIUM SP.

There is still some dispute among mycologists as to whether the various types of fusareums, which are invariably found in connection with nearly all described wilt diseases, are not imperfect forms of the wilt, may never be settled. This, however, we do know, that it attacks the root system of the plant, wilting cotton, cowpeas, peanuts, soybeans, okra, flax, ginseng; and a number of other plants show the greatest infection on the stems just above the ground, often touching and extending down into the ground.

With the peanut, the stems, pegs, and nuts are all affected, often causing the stems to slough away and the nuts to rot.

SCLEROTINIA, SP.

This is one of the most destructive of the peanut diseases, very common and destructive to many plants, especially during long rainy periods. It attacks a great many plants. Up todate the writer has collected it on fifty-two (52) different herbaceous plants.

With the peanut its favorite point of attack seems to be just at the top of the ground. A white mould is readily seen on the ground and stems. It soon girdles the plant causing it to wilt and die. The roots, stems, pegs are affected, under favorable conditions, masses of round shot like bodies can be seen, first white, then brown, and the majority of them about the size of bird shot.

This disease makes the stems and pegs very brittle, and if the vines are pulled the pegs break off leaving a larger percentage of the nuts in the ground. This disease discolores the pods and causes rotting of the kernets also.

Diplodia Sp.? (May be a Spaeropsis)

This disease seems to be growing in importance on account of its destructive habits. This wilt also attacks the roots, stems, and nuts of the peanut, causing numerous dark, warty excresences on the parts attacked. The plant wilts quickly and begins to decay. When the stem is broken the interior has a dark bluish appearance. There are great masses of dark brown spores present.

The same or a similar disease is found on the roots, stems, and boll of cotton, and was collected on the roots and stems of two species of coffee weed, Cassia Tora, and Cassia Marilandica. These plants were growing in the same field with the affected plants.

At the present time the above diseases are the only ones that demand especial attention from every peanut grower. I say at the present time, because the intensive culture of any crop opens the way for a number of new diseases. It also emphasizes the fact that every peanut grower must ever be on the alert to discover and study ways and means of totally eradicating or reducing these diseases to the minimum, so that the quantity and quality of both the nuts and hay will not be seriously affected.

PREVENTATIVE MEASURES

The above diseases were found to be the most destructive where the ground had been poorly prepared, fertilized, and cultivated.

Do not plant peanuts on land where cotton or cow peas wilted badly, the year before, as the peanut is subject to the same wilt.

There are several other diseases to which we are giving attention, but at present seem to be of minor importance.

We urge every farmer to examine his crop frequently and at the first appearance of wilting, yellowing or any abnormal condition of the plants, get in touch with your county agent who will be glad to visit your field and give you whatever help he can.

Respectfully submitted

G. W. Carver, Director

Agricultural Research and Experiment Station[141]

WHILE CARVER WAS GENERATING his report on peanut diseases, Barry was completing the first copy of his bulletin on the culture of Virginia peanuts in the Southeast. He sent a copy to Carver, asking him to look over it and comment before letting it go any further. He alerted Carver that section "G" was left blank so that Barry could include ". . . the reply from all the parties to his letter asking them for any data they have accumulated in the 1930 growing season, if any." Asking Carver to make any notations in pencil directly on the sheet, Barry stated that he would make the corrections. He also asked Carver to make any note ". . . where you feel like the party mentioned might be offended and suggest how to change it." Attached to the letter was a copy of a memo with a handwritten note at the top:

Dr. Carver: - This is memo that would go to Messrs Huston & Richards with copy of Bulletin

Barry

Barry's draft memo continued:

The attached bulletin will give a great deal of data on the culture of the Virginia type peanuts in the Southeast.

Of necessity it is bulky, being the brief of a file about 6 inches thick.

This bulletin is not intended for publication. It goes only to the men who are conducting experiments with peanuts, in Government positions and with private industries, working along the same lines.

Our conclusions and plans have been withheld until Dr. Carver, Grady and myself can get together and make a study of it, over a several day period, point by point. Absolute concentration of thought, on each and every feature, will be necessary to proceed with intelligence and lack of lost motion. Will supply these plans as soon as possible.

After you read it over you will see what a tremendous amount of work it represents. Also how much there is yet to be done.

Dr. Carver and Grady have put in much interested effort. We will continue and have high hopes.

Would like to know what you think of it. [142]

The bulletin, with its partner on the Small Spanish peanut, and Carver's "Diseases of the Peanut," was the backbone of the plan which would be the education awareness component for the growers and stakeholders. The importance of Carver's publication cannot be understated. It also was the critically important, yet controversial at times, centerpiece for the public relations blitz that was to come in the next few months. The objective was for the Tom Huston Company to publish a package that would include: "The Problem"—a set of reports based on thorough scientific data collections, clearly stating the problem for both the Small Spanish peanut and the Virginia peanut—and Carver's report as the "Solution to the Problem."

Porter was still out in the field and wrote Carver that he was sending him some specimens displaying symptoms of "sour heart" from the Alabama Runners they had previously discussed. He cautioned Carver that he would notice the skins on the lesser damaged ones were in good condition. In the same box, Porter noted that he had included a few young Austrian Pear plants that "just don't look right," stating that they came from the same place as the Spanish peanut came from last year, that were so badly affected[143]

The next day, Barry responded to Carver's notice that he had found another disease on the specimens of Alabama Runner peanuts sent over to him by Porter. He said, "The further we go the bigger it gets and the more interesting. I don't know what we would have done without you."[144]

On the following day, Barry sent Carver an edited final copy of Carver's peanut diseases bulletin and asked him to review and approve or make suggestions. He also attached a circular letter he wanted to send out under Carver's name, attached to Carver's bulletin, and asked for Carver's permission to do so. Further, he explained his previous impression:

. . . that it was too early to tell the farmers anything about peanut diseases for fear they would cut the acreage too much. However Mr. Porter and I have talked it over pretty thoroughly and we believe that it would be alright to send your bulletin out right away if a letter is attached similar to the one I am sending in an effort to control their feelings in the matter. On our last visit to you we talked about sending it out about the time farmers were buying seed. Now I believe that we should let it go out right away. Some of the farmers are even now preparing their land and as this bulletin stresses well prepared land and clean seed beds the information cannot get to them too soon.

When we get the papers back with your comments and corrections we will have our letter and your report run off and sent out to 3000 or 4000 right away.[145]

Two weeks later, Barry wrote Carver:

We are now having 5,000 copies of your report on peanuts diseases run off for distribution. With your permission they will go out with the circular letter which I sent you to peanut growers, shelling plants, county agents in the peanut belts of Alabama, Georgia and Florida, both white and colored, to all the newspapers in the peanut belt, to all the banks and to the Extension Service in the Southeastern Peanut Belt and to Washington. Will be glad to send you as many copies as you wish. How many can you use? In this connection please be advised that Mr. Richards read the whole thing over and was of the opinion that it would be effective.

I thank you for correcting and returning my bulletin on Virginia peanuts in the Southeast and would like to be sure that everything in it suits you alright and that you have no objection to us sending out copies to anybody who is in position to do some work along this line. There are about twenty parties referred to in the bulletin and we now have permission from all of them except five to use any data which they have supplied . . . Then if you think the bulletin is alright I will have about 100 copies run off and supply you with as many of them as you want. Already there are other parties becoming interested in that line of work who are in position to get something done. Mr. Cammack, the agricultural agent of the Seaboard railroad at Savannah, spent half a day in my office last week. He states that the Virginia type peanuts are being raised in Bullock County near Savannah and that this type is about the only kind they raise. Hence he is interested and able to do something and I believe that a man of that type should have a copy of the bulletin. Don't you?

I hope that this bulletin has been worded in such a way that both you and ourselves will get full credit for what we have done. Did you see anything in it that could be claimed unfairly by the other parties? I hope that you will be perfectly frank in your remarks always with me because that is what I want and is very necessary to prevent lost motion by both of us.

I am glad to have your letter of the 1st explaining to me more fully the meaning of some of the technical words and abbreviations. I understand it much better now . . .

There is no particular hurry for us to make a study of the Virginia bulletin because the Virginia peanuts won't be planted until April and it won't be a part of the farmers work except those few we select. However I am rushing the Spanish data to them as fast as I can. If you prefer Mr. Porter and I could come over and spend the day with you at Tuskegee and talk the thing over pretty thoroughly. Would that suit you better?[146]

During the first week of February, Barry reported that Porter wanted to go back to Virginia to look at fields, but the Tom Huston Company was so busy buying peanuts that Porter could not be spared as he was needed to locate more tonnage in the field. As soon as Porter was caught up, he could certainly make the trip. A few days later, Porter was able to visit both Virginia and North Carolina. Barry wrote Carver to update him on Porter's trip.

When Mr. Porter was in the Virginia-North Carolina peanut section the last time, he measured off near Tarboro, N.C. 10 feet square in a peanut field which had been harvested. He gathered the peanuts which were left in the ground and they amounted to 2 lbs 14 oz on this 100 square feet. This would be 1251.3 lbs to the acre. So you see that they are having the same trouble up there that we are but don't seem to know it.

Mr. Porter sent me this 2 lbs 14 oz of peanuts . . . I mailed them to you so that you could see what has happened to them in this length of time.

Best personal regards and I hope that your work is letting up on you some.[147]

Since the plant was now receiving peanuts on a daily basis, these would be welcomed since they could certainly provide samples to add to their database. Barry selected samples and sent them to Carver. He was surprised when Carver reported that they were in good condition. He told Carver that he and Porter had made a thorough physical analysis of samples from all the Virginia peanuts shipped into the Tom Huston plant. They could now begin to put their findings into a report, which he had attached as a draft (a narrative and a table) for Carver to review, stating the intent to incorporate this information into the bulletin on the Virginia peanuts.[148]

Attachments: 2

The following tables will show the quality of the Va. Peanuts raised in the Southeast, by the Tom Huston Peanut Co., in 1930.

The general opinion has been that kernels cannot be put in the Va. type peanuts in the Southeast. That if there are any kernels at all they will be damaged.

The table shows that our Va. Runners had 66.0% of kernels in the whole nut and that 65.0% of these kernels were sound. If the lot is eliminated which was dug up from the ground this would have been 65.0% of which 76.5% would be sound.

The Bunch showed 66.6% kernels in the whole nuts, of which 80.0% were sound.

It was a season favorable to the peanut diseases. With a better season or with disease control this would be improved considerably.

The shells on these peanuts look as good as the average Va. type farmers stock. On 1 lot, raised in River bottom silt soil the shells look like they have been polished. In 1 lot raised in red clay, the shells are too red, with clay, for the parching trade.

We arrived at the figures in the table as follows:-

Took a representative sample from many bags of the farmers stock as shipped into us, on each lot, and mixed each sample up good.

Reached in the sample and took out a handful of pods and counted them, good and bad together. Did this several times until we had 100 pods from each lot, taken at random. Weighed the 100 pods.

Removed half the shell from each 100 pods, spread them out on the table and looked them over carefully.

Made a record of the number of pods, from each 100 pods, which were double seeded pops, single seeded pops, one ends, with 2 small kernels, with 1 large and 1 small kernel, with 2 large kernels and three podded. Then the figure in each division is the percent.

Then took the kernels from each 100 pods and counted them and divided into the number of sound kernels, slightly damaged kernels, badly damaged kernels and worthless kernels. Divided each division by the total number of kernels to get the percent in each division.

Weighed kernels from each 100 pods and divided by the weight of the pods, before shelling, to get the percentage of kernels in pods, by weight.

Counted the number of kernels in each 100 pods and added the number that should have been in the pops, one-ends, etc. to get the number that would represent perfection, in so far as the number of kernels are concerned. For it to be perfection in reality, all the kernels would have to be large and also sound.

Last Spring we made an analysis of the seed that was planted and this table [following] shows the comparison of the seed planted and the peanuts made from them for both the Va. Runners and the Va. Bunch.

[Note: Table is not included, as it listed individual farmers' names.]

4

The Plan Is Working

"With a handful of peanuts, Tom was a prophet of profits that benefited Columbus and Georgia."
—"Tom Huston—Fact or Fancy"[149]

"Thank God I love humanity; complexion doesn't interest me one single bit."
—GEORGE WASHINGTON CARVER[150]

At last, the big moment had arrived. The culmination of months of work by the Tom Huston folks and Carver. The plan was definitely in action and producing exciting results! In a February 27, 1931, letter—on a sheet that had printed at the bottom: "By the use of cotton stationery we are helping the southern farmer. Why don't you?"—Bob Barry wrote Carver that:

> Our circular letter, with your disease bulletin, went out to 5,000 different farmers, county agents, experiment stations, banks and newspapers in the southeastern states. I have had some very complimentary replies from some. Some have simply acknowledged it. Some have ignored it and one criticized it very severely, without mincing any words. I want to talk to you about that when I see you.
>
> The sixty page bulletin on Virginia peanuts in the southeast is now being prepared, and I will have about 200 copies of that run off. It will not be sent to the public, but only to those few who can actually do some work to further the cause, until it gets to the point where the farmers can make use of it.
>
> The recent circular letter has caused a great many people to write me and

ask where they could get cotton stationery. So it must be doing some good along that line.

Barry attached copies of the documents that had been sent out:

1) A fact sheet, "Seed Peanuts: This Is the Way We Produce Them";
2) A general circular letter from Barry explaining the devastating effects of peanut diseases, introducing Carver and crediting his work with Tom Huston Peanut Company; and
3) A copy of Carver's report: "Some Peanut Diseases." This document was based on his work and the data from others who also published their similar experiences [see Appendix C]. [151]

Following up on March 9 on his comment in the earlier letter that mentioned that one respondent had criticized Carver's qualifications as a collaborator in the Tom Huston work, Barry wanted to expand that comment and prepare Carver for the viciousness of the character attack by a professional person who had never met Carver. Barry offered his advice:

. . . Like yourself I believe that the disease bulletin is going to do lot of good. I suppose that plant pathology is like most everything else. One doctor might say you have the "Flu" and another might call it the "Grippe" but the one that makes you well is the fellow you want. So I hope you will not become discouraged if some of the scientists do not agree with you or call things by different names . . . [152]

Barry included a copy of a February 19, 1931, letter from Georgia Experiment Station botanist B. B. Higgins. It is apparent that Barry had held the letter until he had an opportunity to study Higgins's comments and prepare Carver for the strongly critical remarks. The entire letter is included here, since it is the first example of the many people, both growers and industry personnel, who cast aspersions on Carver's skills, knowledge, or participation in this project. Also, Barry recognized that Carver was a highly educated yet shy, humble, and quiet man who only wanted to help the farmers in the South.

February 19, 1931

Dear Mr. Barry:

This morning I received the report "Some Peanut Diseases" by Dr. Geo W. Carver, and your accompanying letter. You did not ask for comments but I shall offer some anyhow.

Regarding your letter, I am sure that you do not intend to make mis-statements but infer that you have been misinformed somewhere. Dr. Carver is not a "mycologist of international fame," neither is he a mycologist of any kind. He is supposed to be a chemist. At any rate he knows nothing about fungi. That is shown by a cursory glance at this report in which every single discussion is wrong.

If your object in distributing this report is to help peanut growers by dis-seminating knowledge concerning peanut diseases you are certainly failing in this intention. If you really wish to disseminate such information you might send out Alabama Bulletin No. 108. This bulletin was written by Dr. F. A. Wolf, an internationally known mycologist, now get a copy and compare it with Carver's report, it will not be necessary for me to point out Carver's errors.

I offer these comments with the kindest regards for all concerned, with the sole object of trying to be helpful.

Yours very sincerely

B. B. Higgins

Botanist [153]

The bulletin number recorded in Higgins's letter is 108. However, in follow-up letters from Barry to Higgins it is correctly referred to as Bulletin No. 180.[154]

In response to Higgins, and in a strong defense of Carver, Barry wrote Higgins on March 14, 1931, and sent copies of both letters to Carver:

Dear Mr. Higgins:

At your recent kind suggestion I have sent for bulletin No 180, put out by Auburn in 1914, on peanut diseases. I have gone thru this bulletin and made an effort to understand it, which is hard for a man like me to do of course.

Dr. Carver's recent bulletin was not intended as an exhaustive scientific treatise on peanut diseases. The object was to give the peanut farmer, in language that he could fairly well understand, enough information to make him realize that it is necessary for him to make a study of peanut disease control. Dr. Carver and myself both know that it was simply scratching the surface as far as the scientific end of it goes. I understood bulletin No 180 as going into the same subject a little bit deeper and I realize that many have done this, including Dr. Carver.

I think your recent criticism was brought out by the right spirit but no doubt you lacked information about the man. I would suggest, in a friendly way, that you look him up in the book entitled "Who's Who in America." Also if you can get the Journal of Mycology Vol. 8 No 62 of June 1902 by W. A. Kellerman, Ph.D., Prof. of Botany at Ohio State University, Columbus, Ohio. Also bulletin No 80 of April 1897 entitled "Science Contributions," which was put out by the Ala. Agricultural Experiment Station of the Agricultural and Mechanical College, Auburn, Ala. Also the booklet "Contributions from the Alabama Biological Survey— I" in which you will fine something about new and noteworthy Alabama Fungi and also new species of Alabama Fungi. If you can get these you will see that Dr. Carver has not only located a great many old Fungi but has discovered some new ones which bear his name. He now has on hand something like a thousand specimans of Fungi and has sent to others four or five thousand specimen.

Dr. Carver feels very friendly towards you and would appreciate a visit. You can see peanut specimen of last year there. We feel that Dr. Carver "Knows his Stuff." In addition to that he is only 60 miles from us and will give us any amount of time, on a few minutes notice, and go anywhere to make investigations. He thoroughly enjoys it. You can readily see how much this means and understand better why we have done so much work with him.

Possibly we have thoughtlessly created the impression that we are ignoring the valuable information worked out by the Experiment Stations, but we have studied all of their bulletins and feel very much indebted to them for a great deal of enlightenment. The troubles of last year required much time and given often, so it was natural for us to turn to the one who could give it. I can appreciate exactly how you feel but hope this letter will make a difference.

Hope to find time to visit you this Summer. Also hope that your Station will continue its good work on peanuts in 1931, and advise us of results.

Good luck.

Cordially yours,

TOM HUSTON PEANUT COMPANY

Bob Barry, Mgr.

Shelling Dept. [155]

Because of Carver's strong spiritual beliefs that had given him strength throughout his life, he could show respect and understanding following the character attack by Higgins. Furthermore, he had always realized that the farmer did not have the technical vocabulary to understand scientific reports, and that is why hundreds of Carver's Bulletins have been requested and reprinted over the years: he wrote them at the level of understanding of the client, the farmer. This is translational science at its best: nontechnical communication to stakeholders, by such a pioneer as Carver.

Carver was very aware of the potential cost to Barry for defending him against the negative insinuations made by Higgins. He realized that Barry could get in serious trouble with his company as well as the farmers his company served, for defending a black person. Yet, he had faith in the total honesty, strength, and depth of his and Barry's relationship; representing an unbroken chain of trust from Carver's original agreement with Tom Huston, his own commitment to Huston's vision, to Huston's appointment of Barry to direct the work of the Team. Thus, Carver would not permit such an issue to dissuade him from his commitment to help the Tom Huston Peanut Company, or the peanut growers, as exemplified in his March 18 letter to Barry:

Thank you so much for a copy of the letter to Mr. B. B. Higgins. It is a masterpiece. Not because you have said those nice things about me, but because you have forecasted the successful development of peanut production as it is only possible through the cooperative efforts of the grower, the Experiment Stations, and specialists along these lines.

I so thoroughly agree with you that Mr. Higgins is not aware of the vast amount of work done last year and how untiring you and Mr. Porter were in your efforts to get information, not only on peanut diseases, but on all phases of peanut production. Neither time nor expense was spared.

You have also hit the keynote when you say the real technical bulletin is beyond the understanding of the average farmer, and if he is to be helped we must talk in his language as far as possible and practicable. Many Experiment Stations recognize this need and often you find bulletins describing diseases as the farmer knows them. A notable example is the designation red rust or black rust of cotton, both of which are utterly valueless to the technical worker, but have become so general in their application by the layman that they convey the idea at once of two unusually destructive cotton diseases, and that he must fight them vigorously if a good crop is expected. This is why some Experiment Stations and other technical workers are writing sets of bulletins especially for the farmer.

I do not wish to minimize the value of technical bulletins and papers as these give to the technical worker exact truths, the only method by which he can work out control methods.

I believe we are going to do much more of this in the future, rendering therefore a greater service to the farmer in all of his various activities.

This letter of yours to Mr. Higgins is a distinct challenge for growth. Are we big enough, broad enough, altruistic enough to catch the vision of bigger and better things for, not only the peanut grower, but the farmer in all of his work which is the very backbone of the nation's progress.

Mr. Barry, I believe your challenge will be accepted by the vast majority.

You are indeed right. I have a very friendly feeling toward Mr. Higgins, and I sincerely hope he will come over and study the situation as it is. I am sure that it is of much greater magnitude with more puzzling ramifications than he has an idea at this time.

I believe, Mr. Barry, that this very bulletin is going to set the pace for other workers. I believe also that you will find the peanut growers giving attention to it and profiting by it.

When much more work is done by the various stations and specialists in cooperation, it will, upon their decision, be time enough for a technical bulletin on peanut diseases. In the meantime, I hope the peanut grower will be furnished information in a nontechnical way that he can understand.

Your letter to Mr. Higgins is the most convincing, sympathetic, high class letter that I have ever read. Only persons possessed with great hearts and souls could write a letter like that.

I am glad you wrote Mr. H. P. Vannah so fully. He is making a real contribution to the peanut grower and has put it in language that they can understand. I have placed it in the folder with the others as you requested.

Thank you for the list of bulletins and papers on peanut diseases. I am going through mine as rapidly as possible.[156]

In the spirit of scientific collaboration which could be beneficial to the farmer, Carver refused to acknowledge the negative insinuations by Higgins and continued to respond and act with positivity. Carver put together and sent to Barry a short memorandum which he hoped would better explain his role and intent, requesting that it be included with any future mailouts or handouts of the *Peanut Diseases* bulletin:

To Whom It May Concern:

This bulletin on peanut diseases is an effort on my part to help the peanut grower, and was not intended from any angle as technical mycological data on diseases.

I just wanted the farmer to know that he has several destructive peanut diseases and some of the ways by which he may combat them.

Yours very truly

G. W. Carver, Director

Agricultural Research & Experiment Station [157]

Barry and Carver felt they had adequately handled, in a profoundly professional way, Higgins's negative charges, and they decided that they would no longer spend valuable time on that issue.

Continuing with data compilation to support their findings, Barry sent Carver a listing of all bulletins that he had used to make any reference to peanut diseases. He said he was aware that there might be more bulletins that he did not know about but would merge his list with Carver's upon receipt. He further shared that he was "surprised to find how little information we have from the Southeastern States," and cautioned that "we want to be more careful about not offending them than anybody else." He told Carver he had requested a copy of every bulletin on peanut diseases used by each Experiment Station in Georgia, Alabama, and Florida.

Mr. Bob Barry,
  Shelling Dept.
Tom Huston Peanut Co.
  Columbus, Ga.

Mar. 23 – 31.

ATTACHED: Typed copy +
Bibliography of
Plant Diseases
ep

My dear Mr. Barry:—

Please find litterature of Plant diseases consulted in the preliminary work on Peanut diseases being sent to the farmers.

There is no doubt new and undescribed diseases affecting the peanut. I have therefore consulted all of these authorities who have dealt with Rhizotonia, Sclerotia Fusarium, Bacterial wilts etc. etc. with the hope that they would throw more light on the subject, and give us a better basis for cooperative work on peanut diseases in the future.

Please look it over carefully. Arrange it all in any form you wish that suits your publications best.

I note you have arranged your li. in one way. (quite systematic).

Above and opposite, Carver's handwritten letter of March 23, 1931, to Bob Barry of the Tom Huston Peanut Company (Courtesy of the Tuskegee University Archives).

mine is rather [2] heterogeneous, as though you would make it sit in just as you wished it.

If you see any duplications, eliminate them.

Very sincerely yours.
G. W. Carver.

[Editor's note: The carbon of this draft below.]

Even more surprising, Barry told Carver, "by looking at the dates you see that Dr. Taubenhaus is the only one who has done any extensive recent work. Naturally he is going to be a big help." J. J. Taubenhaus was chief of the division of plant pathology & physiology at Texas A & M University and the Texas Agricultural Experiment Station. In closing, Barry said, "There is a whole lot of work to it but I believe it is well worth it. Don't you?"[158]

On March 23, 1931, Carver sent Barry his list of literature on plant diseases, organized by state, that were consulted in the preliminary work on peanut diseases being sent to the farmers. Included was Carver's publication, Bulletin No. 4, 1901: "Some Cercospora of Macon County, Alabama." Carver wrote:

> There are, no doubt, new and undescribed diseases affecting the peanut, I have therefore, consulted all of these authorities who have dealt with Rhizotonia, Sclerotinia, Fusarium, Bacterial wilts, etc., with the hope that they will throw more light on the subject and give us a better basis for cooperative work on peanut diseases in the future.
>
> Please look it over carefully and arrange it all in any form you wish that suits your publication best.
>
> I note you have arranged your list in one way (quite systematic). Mine is rather heterogeneous, as I thought you would make it fit in just as you wished it. If you see any duplications eliminate them.[159]

In an exciting development, one of Barry's inquiries had received a reply from Dr. Paul Tabor, professor of farm crops at the State College of Georgia at Athens. Barry responded that Tabor's letter was "the best news I have had in a long time." Also, it is interesting that he included praise for B. B. Higgins and the assistance he had rendered to this point. He wrote that he was:

> delighted to know Mr. E. D. Alexander is perfecting arrangements with the railroad agricultural agents and with Prof. Miller of the University of Georgia to conduct a survey of peanut diseases over the Southern part of Georgia for several years.

If you have no objection I would like to pass this information on to the Southeastern Peanut Association, which includes practically all of the peanut shellers and crushers in the Southeast.

Referring to bulletins on peanut diseases please be advised that we are now making a list of a number of bulletins from the United States and foreign countries which touch on peanut diseases and diseases related to them.

Mr. Higgins of the Georgia Experiment Station has contributed a great deal along these lines and will no doubt be one of the most valuable men in working out disease control. We have several articles written by him.

We conducted a 28 acre tract of Small Spanish peanuts last year and will be glad to send you a copy of our report on it if you wish. From it you can get some good information about the effect of weather on diseases.

We will be delighted to render you any assistance that we can along these lines but realize that since you have made these wonderful plans you will learn more about it than we ever will know.

It would be a pleasure to have you come to see us sometime.[160]

At the top, he wrote in pencil, "Copy to Dr. Carver." The significance of this announcement was that it accomplished one step in the Plan: that of getting some financial support and involved work by a recognized researcher.

Barry wrote Carver on the following day:

Both Mr. Porter and myself feel entirely too ignorant on these peanut diseases, especially in regard to what others have done along these lines. We have been discussing the matter and have been wondering if it would be asking too much of you to take some of your time every week and go over these various bulletins in your presence. There are so many things in them that you could straighten us out on. Then too all three of us would have so much better idea about how to handle the other fellows. Some of the bulletins just have a paragraph or two on diseases and a great many of them could be disposed of in a hurry. There are others that would take a great deal longer.

We do not want to be greedy with your time so please think it over and tell us whether you believe it is worth while or not. We will need plenty of ammunition before the fight is over.[161]

On the same day, after receiving a letter from Carver, Barry wrote again:

... I am trying to get another copy of bulletin No 180 from Auburn so that you can have one for your file. If I fail to get it there I'll try to get it somewhere else.

I have had the introduction to the Virginia peanut bulletin re-run. When we get the bibliography together it will be ready to go out. Then we'll have some interesting letters.

The World is small after all. Apples and pears in Italy suffering with the same disease as Runner peanuts in Alabama. I have never seen the Tricho-thecium roseum that you refer to and hope that I can take a look with the microscope the next time I come over. We will sure go into that a little bit deeper this Summer.

Mr. Porter expects to bring the Ft. Gaines county agent over to see you sometime this week. I believe that we can put things into his head that will be contagious alright . . .[162]

In a follow-up letter to Carver, Barry wrote:

The Va. bulletin will be ready to go out about Tuesday. The Bibliography should tie in with as many peanut diseases as possible, don't you think?

What do you think of my putting in the bulletin somewhere, with a rubber stamp, that since it was printed you have found that Trichothecium Roseum has been found on the Ala. Runner and is no doubt causing the "sour heart." Also refer to any other diseases that you have found later on peanuts.

Beleive that we should give the other fellows as much to look for as possible. Also the less local the data is, the more interest Washington will take in it.

If you favor this please write me just how to word it. Believe you said that you found Pericularia Grisea on the Ala. Runner also, didn't you?

Anything you say. Thanks.[163]

Attached to this letter was the edited copy of *Bibliography, Peanut Diseases and Those Related to Them*, organized by state, country, and date of publication. A note at the end stated that the "list was taken from the files of Dr. Geo. W. Carver of Tuskegee Institute, Tuskegee, Alabama, and from the files of the Tom Huston Peanut Co., of Columbus, Georgia."

During this time and according to the plan, Barry and Porter had been putting together a document of their findings, entitled *Peanuts* [see cover, page 21]. Carver received his copy and wrote to thank Barry:

This is to acknowledge the receipt of and to thank you for your rich magazine entitled PEANUTS. It is clear, concise and exquisitely illustrated. It is so far ahead of anything that I have seen on peanuts, that I see nothing to criticize, but everything to commend.

This book can and, I am sure, will be used in many schools and by everyone who wants the last word in the production of the white Spanish variety of peanuts. The farmer will find it invaluable.

The vast amount of experimental work that you and Mr. Porter have outlined will no doubt give you valuable data to add to some of the topics.

Again thanking you for this unusually fine publication, I am

Yours very sincerely,

G. W. Carver, Director

Agricultural Research and Experiment Station[164]

A few days later Carver wrote Barry again, attaching three more references to insert in the *Bibliography, Peanut Diseases and Those Related to Them*:

With the vast amount of work we have already done and what we have outlined for this year's work, together with the challenges you have thrown out, the cooperative interest you have awakened, I believe we going to make monumental strides along the line of peanut diseases and their control.

This bibliography ought to supplement what they already have in an admirable way.

Since you and Mr. Porter have shown such ability in the recognition of peanut diseases, I am wondering if it would be asking too much of you, with all of your other duties, to get a working knowledge of these diseases. We will group them by great families, then subdivide each great family into smaller groups. I know you will find it easy. You will find it exceedingly interesting to get acquainted with host plants in the same way. By fall you will know all the described ones.

Now is the time to look for Peronosporas, the downy fungus found on the underside of the leaves of several plants. It is usually white in color, but a few species are smoke brown.

The Aecidiums are known as cluster cups, because they resemble little tubes somewhat. They too are usually found on the underside of the leaves of many plants, giving them a similar diseased appearance to that caused by the Peronosporas.

The Cedar Apple fungus is also ready. Some of the limbs and stems are diseased also.

At present I doubt if we should say anything about the Trichothecium roseum (Pers) Link, Cephalothecium roseum Corda, Dactylium roseum, B.

I have some inoculation experiments going on now. I am not sure it is the cause of sour heart, we will have to work it out this summer.

The only thing we would be safe in saying is that Trichothecium roseum has been found in the "sour hearted" peanuts and that further studies were being made to find out definitely if it had any connection with the so called "sour heart." (It may be an excellent thing to put this in. I am saving some to show you when you come over).[165]

The next week, Barry wrote to let Carver know that the Virginia bulletin was ready to go out and Barry was trying to make up a mailing list. Copies would go to the Experiment Stations in Alabama, Florida, Georgia, and South Carolina. To protect the team's discoveries and findings, Barry preferred not to send copies to Virginia or North Carolina to preserve a weapon with which to "fight us off of their monopoly."

... Am in question about the Experiment Stations in Texas, Oklahoma, Miss. Arkansas and La. They no doubt have some men who can be of a great deal of value in so far as the diseases are concerned. Neither are they trying to raise the Virginia peanut out there. Maybe it would be alright to send them copies. What do you think?

Then there are the men in Washington who could get in behind the Stations and make them do something. I am inclined to want to send them some but would they pass them on to the Va. Stations? If they did could it hurt us much? Please say what you think about this.

I would like to send one to each County Agent in the Peanut Belt of Ga., Ala. & Fla. Do you see any objection to this?

Please give me your opinion about each Section as soon as you can so I can let the Bulletin go on out.

Mr. Porter's wife have been at the point of death with pneumonia and his baby has the Influenza. They are reported much better today, I am glad to say.

We will run over to see you again as soon as we can.[166]

Barry received a copy of a general letter sent to active members of the Southeastern Peanut Association. This letter is included in its entirety because of the exciting message, indicating that the team was nearing the overall goal of getting targeted people to take notice.

April 4, 1931
Circular No. 26
Peanut Diseases
ACTIVE MEMBERS:
As a follow up to our Circular letter No. 25 of March 17th I wish to quote for your further information a letter from Mr. Bob Barry, Manager Shelling Department, Tom Houston Peanut Company, Columbus, Ga., 2nd instant reading as follows:

"I am glad to be able to quote from a letter of March 20th, 1931 from Mr. Paul Tabor, Professor of Farm Crops, State College of Agriculture, University of Georgia Athens, Georgia.

'In regard to peanut diseases our extension agronomist, Mr. E. D. Alexander, is perfecting arrangements with the railroad agricultural agents and with Prof. J. H. Miller of the University of Georgia, to conduct a survey of peanut diseases over the southern part of Georgia for several years.'

I believe all of the members of our association will be glad to get this news and I am sending it to them through you. Mr. Tabor has given me permission to broadcast this news.

It would be a fine thing if all of the shellers would write to Mr. Tabor and thank him for making these plans. It would help him a great deal if all of them would offer to cooperate with the State College of Agriculture in their particular section."

Hoping you will find it entirely consistent to act upon his suggestion to the extent of communicating with Mr. Tabor on the subject, I am,

Yours very truly,

S. LINTHICUM

SECRETARY - TREASURER [167]

As a follow up to his April 3 letter to Carver, after receiving Carver's comments as requested, Barry wrote him on April 6, to finalize the list of names to be sent the Virginia bulletins. Copies were going to the Experiment Stations in Alabama, Georgia, Florida, and South Carolina.

. . . I also sent one to the Brown Company in the Everglades because they furnished so much valuable information. I also sent one to Mr. J. H. Beattie at Washington because he seems to be in close touch with all of the Experiment Stations in the Southeast . . .

Mr. Porter and myself think that we should not send out any more to anybody except to the County Agents of Georgia, Alabama and Florida in the biggest peanut counties. He thinks that it would be alright for you to send a copy to Dr. Taubenhaus or anybody else in the Southwest who can and will really be of service. If you think well of this I will not send out any more but will supply you with any number you wish.

I sent one to Dr. Herty in New York City and attached a memorandum asking him to go over it before he talked to the Washington officials. He will no doubt do this.[168]

The journey was on the verge of its most exciting and rewarding time. The plan had existed for almost a year and a half, and the team had accomplished several goals, especially in increased awareness of peanut diseases among targeted individuals and groups. Peanut growth and disease data had been carefully and diligently collected; an ever-expanding number of the peanut growers/farmers in the Southeast had been visited; research findings had been published in educational pamphlets, booklets, and informational letters; and a multilayered mailing list had been developed which included farmers, researchers, Extension agents, trade organizations, and local, state, and federal government officials. The interest in and understanding of the problem had initiated conversations among stakeholders who previously had neither connected nor shared information with each other.

With the groundwork now firmly in place, the team could take time to evaluate what had been accomplished and what still needed to be done to achieve the goal of the new plan. The team would continue gathering peanut growth and disease data to increase the database; expand the scope of the educational outreach component by increasing the number of presentations at professional meetings and fairs; initiate publication of educational materials in respected trade journals; and, importantly, add a focus on wives of peanut farmers. Much work for the three-man team would be required in the coming months to ensure that these activities were successfully accomplished.

They had spent hours assisting the growers in understanding and identifying problems with peanut diseases and crop health, while offering advice and solutions at no charge. The arrangement for Professor J. H. Miller of the University of Georgia to conduct the multiyear survey of peanut diseases was a real breakthrough, since he had a link to interest at the federal level—the ultimate goal. The team of Barry, Porter, and Carver was committed to continue its efforts to attract the attention and support of federal researchers. The latter was considered critical to the survival of the peanut industry, because it was the team's belief that until those at the federal level recognized the problems caused by peanut diseases, funds would not be provided for the aid of farmers in the peanut-growing sections of the country.

5

The Plan Begins to Bear Fruit

*My greatest desire is to make a contribution to education
which will last throughout all time, to me no amount of
money is even comparable to that idea.*
— GEORGE WASHINGTON CARVER[169]

B ob Barry wrote Carver on April 7, 1931, thanking him for his willingness
to go over the bulletins in detail with himself and Porter:

> Both of us need this and will we be very glad to get it. When I was ten years
> old I didn't think I would still be going to school at forty three but I surely am,
> and enjoying it . . .
>
> I know that if you do we will have our peanut guns loaded with more effective
> ammunition . . .
>
> All of us over here appreciate your fine co-operation and see all kind of signs
> of it's bearing much fruit for the peanut grower and the industry as a whole. We
> sure took our troubles to the right man.[170]

Carver wrote Barry that he had planted some of the spotted peanuts
that Grady Porter had brought on his last visit to Tuskegee:

> . . . I planted a number of the spotted peanuts that Mr. Porter brought over
> when he was here last. I presume you know about them. They are the peanuts
> that have the dark brown spots on them. Some of them sprouted but seem
> very weak. Some I placed on top of the clean sand and simply put a covering
> over the vessel containing them. Many of these germinated also, but weak.
> A number of them developed the Trichothecium-simply covered them with

pink spores. I am saving them for you and Mr. Porter to see. Of course, there were other moles, but small quantities in proportion to the Trichothecium. I am greatly interested in this fungus and shall make a number of other tests. I believe that we are on the right road to finding something worth while with reference to this spotted condition and the sour heart also . . . [171]

On April 16, Barry wrote Carver about the disappointing spring germination rate of the peanut seeds:

This Spring we have been very much disappointed in the low percentage of germination in all peanuts for seed. The various Experiment Stations have run germination tests for me and the average of all of them is somewhere between 75% and 80%. The last two previous years run way up in the nineties.

They say the low percentage of germination is due to so many peanuts having mould on the shell. They do not seem to consider that the peanut diseases of last year have anything to do with it. They are more inclined to believe that the peanuts become moulded in the stacks and that this mould rots the kernel before it germinates or makes a weak germination. Some of them shelled a few and ran a germination test on them both shelled and unshelled. The shelled seed proved better.

I am sending you a few of the moulded peanuts which I have picked out of the seed pile and would like to have you advise just what you think causes the unsatisfactory condition.[172]

THE BIG PUBLICATION PR BLITZ IS LAUNCHED!

Because of the apparent lack of understanding of the cause of peanut diseases, Barry felt the time was critical if the peanut industry is to survive. The team now had enough information on the diseases and the problems faced by the growers and the industry and had made enough contacts to integral players in this situation. The time was right to put into motion the last piece of the plan, the media blitz [see Appendix B].

In a letter to Carver, Barry wrote:

I would like to see something about peanuts diseases in every issue of the trade papers until action is forced.

Believe that the attached would be alright for the nest issue. I could send it along or if you prefer to, it will suit us alright.

If you approve of it, and want me to send it in, please make any additions or corrections that occur to you.

It might be well for you to be thinking up similar articles for future editions.[173]

Meanwhile, Barry and Porter continued to monitor the growth of peanuts in the fields and had devised a plan to assist growers for the next season. He sent Carver the information and a copy of the list of seed types:

We are enclosing a list of seventy-five different kinds of peanuts which we have on hand for seed.

These peanuts were raised on our Experiment Farm in Columbus, Ga., which is not operating this season.

This letter and list is going to all of the Government Experiment Stations. We will be glad to supply any of them 6 to 12 seed of each kind for their experimental work, without charge.

The supply will of course go to those who ask for them first, as long as they last. There is only about a handful of each.[174]

Bas-relief plaque presented to George Washington Carver by Tom Huston in 1931.

By May 15, Barry was receiving responses from the Experiment Stations to the circular sent out offering farmers samples of peanut seeds. He was very pleased that twelve stations had ordered the sets.

Carver received a letter from Barry letting him know that he had made a trip to their Experimental Station Tract in Fort Gaines, Georgia, and had examined the plants there. Barry told Carver that while the oldest planting of April 25th was doing really well, he was concerned that the youngest plants were showing much leaf spot disease. In fact, he had never seen this much disease on plants this young. Since he knew little about this disease, he asked Carver for answers to the following questions:

"No. 1 - Is there anything we can do in this field [for] the balance of the season to help the situation?

No. 2 - Just what is the nature of the damage we might expect from this disease?

No. 3 - Is it apt to effect the peanuts or just the hay?

No. 4 - If it will effect the peanuts materially please explain in just what way."

He invited Carver to visit the fields if he could find the time.[175]

On May 26, Barry wrote again to Carver and suggested, "If you can get some of the other pathologists to work with you on various diseases like Dr. Sherbakoff is on Fusariums it will do you both and the industry a lot of good." He offers any help he could give. He told Carver that, "The letter on leaf spot was sent to Mr. Higgins at Experiment, Georgia, Mr. Vannah at Belle Glade, Fla., and Mr. Seal at Auburn, Ala.," but he had received no replies.[176]

During the spring commencement exercises at Tuskegee in May 1931, Carver was presented with a bas-relief plaque commissioned by Tom Huston from the artist Isabell Shultz. Huston was unable to attend but wrote Carver:

I am sending to you by Bob Barry and Grady Porter, who know you so well and admire you so much, the Bronze likeness of yourself. It is by Isabell Schultz.

You have contributed much to an industry that is close to our hearts, thereby endearing yourself to us all. This Bronze is a small token of our appreciation. To look at it is to receive inspiration. Surely it must inspire workers of the future just as you have inspired those who have been fortunate enough to work with you.

It is disappointing that I was not able to present it to you in person. I have looked forward to it. But I thought it best to send it rather than delay longer.[177]

Barry made the presentation on Huston's behalf, saying that Huston does not like publicity in person and has been busy with his new venture into frozen foods. Afterwards, Carver wrote both men to thank them for the plaque and the comments made during the presentation and to tell them how much he and Tuskegee Institute President Robert R. Moton appreciated not only the gift but the spirit behind it.[178]

Barry responded:

. . . The delivery was, as you said, void of oratory. I knew that. The lesson in it is that sincerety is greater than oratory. The people heard a voice and knew that the mind was directing the voice but it originated in the heart. There was no effort on my part. It was simply an expression of what I really felt and that is why it went over, without the oratorical frills.

Dr. Moton saw the significance of it when he said, after I had finished, that it was deeper than it appeared on the surface. That it had a great deal of meaning for a very busy Southern gentleman to spend his time and money to so honor a "black man."

It will be even more significant when I tell you that I am the grandson of a Confederate Major who went through the whole War, but afterwards started off the great colored Missionary, to Africa, Dr. Shepard, on the right track when he was only a boy. My other grandfather was killed in the War. Sherman's army came to Savannah and destroyed everything on this grandfather's plantation, leaving his wife with 5 young children to raise alone. She had to make everything for them, even their shoes. I am from this seed and you know the rest.

To your people this should prove that the man within is greater than his skin. Many of my race also have that lesson to learn.

I feel good about it all and I know you do.[179]

Barry wrote Carver for a copy of his 1901 bulletin on the leaf spot and suggested that they start now in selecting the specimens for Barry's and Carver's offices, referring to the spaces as "herbariums." Those would be diseased plants to be used for education purposes. A small museum was planned for the lobby of the Tom Huston plant in Columbus, and Barry had asked Carver to provide a small bottle of each of the products he had made from peanuts. These would be displayed with the Huston company's copy of the bronze plaque.[180] The museum's display cases were to be designed and stained with formulas developed by Carver and built by the Tom Huston Company folks. Barry felt that these would be an inspiration to the thousands of visitors each year and would also amplify Carver's work on the team's project.

Barry wrote Carver a second letter dated May 15, updating him on the status of their plan:

> The Government Experiment Stations are responding very nicely to my recent circular letter and twelve of them have already ordered a set of the 75 different kinds of peanuts. I am keeping a small jar of each myself.
>
> We already have about a hundred different kinds of peanuts mounted in attractive glass cases which we are saving for our museum.
>
> I am glad to know that Prof. Sherbakoff is doing some active work with the specimens which you are sending to him. I have written to Dr. Hertyte [to] find out just what pathologist in Washington will do the same thing so that we can send him specimens all along. It is interesting to know that the Senior Micologist at Washington has sent for one of the peanut bulletins.
>
> Yes they are getting to work alright. Almost any kind of an egg will hatch if you set on it long enough, won't it.[181]

Barry continues to work with Porter and the growers to gather information during the growing season. He made another trip to Fort Gaines, Georgia, and collected specimens that Porter would send to Carver. Then, in an effort to keep working with the south Alabama growers, he and Porter went to Headland, Alabama. There they visited with the superintendent of the Wiregrass Experiment Station, who had a small patch of peanuts but had not been very interested in peanuts prior to now because he was a cotton man. However, he did request several strains of seed and indicated that he would try a bigger patch next year. Barry also apprised Carver that he was pleased with the article on peanut diseases in the *Peanut World,* and it was the only one related to the Tom Huston Company project. He offered congratulations that Carver and Dr. Sherbakoff were cooperating so nicely. [182]

Not forgetting his earlier request to Carver to teach him and Grady Porter more about the peanut, Barry wrote that he would like to know more "about the peanuts (*sic*) little individual laboratory." He felt that he and Grady could provide better responses to questions asked of them in the increasing numbers of presentations and meetings with the growers and professional colleagues if they had a greater understanding of the biology and chemistry of the growth cycle of the plant. He explained to Carver that:

> . . . Always I am wondering what the leaves consist of; the stems; the roots; the pegs; the hulls; the kernel. Then I wonder where the plant got these various ingredients, what form they were originally in and what changes were made in taking material from something else and giving it to the plant in its proper form. Also what happens when it is deficient in any one of its requirements.
>
> Could you get me right on this or is that asking too much? [183]

Following Barry and Porter's trip to Fort Gaines, Barry invited Carver to visit and discuss with Porter what method of control should be used. Carver did make the visit, and he and Porter made detailed plans for the best method to control the leaf spot. Barry found it very interesting that Carver had found Fusarium on the kernels of the peanuts which they had sent over to Tuskegee. He asked Carver if that was the first case of Fusarium on the kernel itself, and he looked forward to Carver completing his incubation tests for proof. To make a point that progress was being made in encouraging the interest of the Agricultural Extension folks, especially in Alabama, Barry caught Carver up on Dr. Marion Jacob Funchess, who came to Alabama Polytechnic Institute (API, now Auburn University) as an assistant professor of agriculture in 1909, was named professor of agronomy in 1915, and served as head of the department 1920–1934.

Mr. Funchess at Auburn has been about the most uninterested agricultur-
alist, in peanut diseases, of them all. I recently sent him a blue print of our
tracts at Ft. Gaines and he has now even expressed a desire to go down there
and visit them. I expect to keep warming some of these donkey eggs until they
hatch out race horses . . .[184]

Barry asked Carver for permission to use his 1901 bulletin on leaf spot
in the industry trade papers because he found it interesting that, although
the information came out thirty years before, the same troubles were still
present. He felt that these diseases had a direct connection to the current
poor stands, and he was glad that Carver would provide the proof.[185]

Barry sent Carver a copy of a memorandum that had been sent to the
names provided on an attached list. The memorandum stated:

Attached you will find a list of the 19 different parties to whom we recently
sent seed of 75 different kinds of peanuts for experimental purposes.
    Some of you will no doubt want to compare notes with others and this is
the object of the information.
    If you will kindly include us in reporting your findings it will be greatly ap-
preciated. [186]

The list included a botanist and a horticulturist from the Bureau of
Plant Industry in Washington, D.C., as well as professors, botanists, plant
pathologists, agronomists, and supervisors of Experiment Stations from
seventeen colleges and universities in the South. Barry shared with Carver
that he was pleased that their efforts had begun to generate interest and
cooperation among this group. He indicated that if these folks continued
to work with the information being produced by the team and the plan,
then the mission would be well on its way to the hoped-for results.

Carver received a letter from Barry letting him know that Mr. Neil E.
Stevens, senior pathologist with the USDA Plant Disease Survey in Washington, D.C., had supplied envelopes to use when sending specimens of
the diseased plants to him. This was a huge milestone! It meant that, at last,
someone at the highest level was willing to work with the team and begin to

establish a data repository at that level. That accomplished one of the main objectives of the plan: to make specific people at the highest level aware of the peanut diseases and the potential for disastrous effects on the economy of this large income crop in the Southeast. Their support was critically needed because they had the power to direct funding to the Southeastern states' Agricultural Extension Services, that ultimately will help the growers.[187]

The supplied envelopes were quickly filled and forwarded to Washington. Excitedly, Barry wrote Carver one week later that "more envelopes have been sent. They are 'Raring' for some more specimens now." [188]

To move a step further in the educational outreach efforts, Barry sent Carver a copy of a letter he had prepared to mail to every Extension agent in the southeastern peanut belt. To encourage continued learning, an incentive was offered to each grower—free peanut publications. Carver had long advocated that farmers subscribe to the latest agricultural publications. In 1917, he had published an article entitled "Twelve Ways to Meet the New Economic Conditions Here in South." No. 11 was: "Will it pay a farmer to take an agricultural paper?" Carver's answer was: "Yes, it is a necessity. He should not only take one or two good agricultural papers, but others as well. He must study markets, crops, weather, supply and demand, and a host of other things which affect him and his business. It is just as important to the farmer as to the merchant. In fact, it is the only way that either can keep abreast of the times."[189]

Barry's letter, attached to his June 11, 1931, letter to Carver, stated:

Peanut Growers have begun to realize that PLANT DISEASES have, in the past, greatly reduced the yield and quality of their PEANUTS.

They want to do something towards working out DISEASE CONTROL. But they need advice.

Who is better equipped to aid them than their friend, the County Agricultural Agent?

In order that you may get the most recent information on this subject, we have subscribed to three peanut magazines, to be sent to you monthly, at our expense.

Every issue will have an article on PEANUT DISEASES. They will be written by many different men who have had recent experience with PEANUT DISEASES. The subject will be taken up from many different angles.

We are sure that you will cooperate.

Cordially yours,

TOM HUSTON PEANUT COMPANY

Bob Barry, Mgr.

Shelling Dept.[190]

Results were coming in faster now, and the team could see positive responses to its carefully planned efforts. Light was visible at the end of the tunnel. Barry wrote to Carver:

Glad to have your two letters of June 8th and 9th. Your letters have become a very important part of my daily doings and if I could keep getting them I will some day be a peanut man. I hope that I am not overburdening you.

I have received letters from a great many of the County Agents to whom we are sending the peanut papers. The very evident tone of appreciation is very gratifying. We could get these boys to step out if the higher-ups were a little bit different.

I am glad to know that you are willing to work with any specimens sent in by Co. Agts. I doubt if they could find anybody else who would do that. Would you object to me sending to all of the trade papers something like the attached sheet? They all need the encouragement. Maybe it would be best for you to send something to the papers like this direct.

Thanks very much for your offer to go into the little peanut's chemical laboratory with us on the next trip. Don't you ever refuse a fellow?

The boys sure did respond to our offer to give them 75 different kinds of peanuts. It is gratifying to know that they are willing to sandwich in some of this kind of work in their program although there are no appropriations for it. What would they do if they were properly backed up. If I'm not mistaken they soon will be. [191]

No sheet was attached in the files. It is possible that Barry referred to the General Letter, previously mentioned, that he mailed to every Extension agent in the southeastern peanut belt. Carver recorded on his copy that he received his "on June 8, 1931." But it is more probable that he was referring to the Memorandum entitled:

TO ALL COUNTY AGENTS IN THE SOUTHEAST

Now that you are becoming interested in recent developments of PEANUT DISEASES, you will want to do some work with the plants themselves, in the fields.

I want you all to feel free to mail to me any specimens that you gather. I will gladly identify the DISEASES, for you, to the best of my ability and report the results.

You should send specimens to other Pathologists also, so that one can check his finding against others.

A general spirit of co-operation by all concerned will soon bear much fruit. You can count on me.

George W. Carver, Director

Research & Experiment Station

Tuskegee Nor. & Ind. Institute,

Tuskegee, Ala [192]

It is significant to note that Barry thanked Carver for offering to work with the specimens brought in by Extension agents, because that meant Carver would expand his research time to assist agents outside Tuskegee's Agricultural Extension responsibility. Carver knew how critically important it was that research should translate into Extension work to benefit the community. In so doing, farmers would become stakeholders with the university and industry. Even today, Extension and Research maintain that vitally important partnership.

Few if any of these Extension agents were black, and few if any had ever worked with Carver on a professional basis, although they might have encountered him at meetings and fairs or perhaps heard one of his presentations. Yet, Carver was willing to share his knowledge, time, and laboratory with them. It is equally significant to realize that Carver received no salary for his contribution to this entire project. Although Carver did receive a July 1929 job offer from Walter Richards, vice president of Tom Huston

Peanut Company, Carver declined the offer. The reason is simple: He saw the need for what he was already doing. Carver had responded to the job offer with this letter:

Mr. Walter A. Richards, Vice President

Tom Huston Peanut Company

Columbus, Ohio

Your letter of June 24" has been received and contents noted with much care.

I have thought much about what you said when in conference in your office, and your letter emphasizes it all the more strongly. I fear however, that the problem is a little more complex than you are aware, as the following points must be considered:

1st. The peanut is only one of the dozens of attractive things with which I have worked.

2nd. And the most delicate to me is the fact that I am an employee of the school and draw my salary from the school, therefore, it reserves the right to at least suggest my movements which, of course, is absolutely right, and a suggestion from my employer is always a direct order to do it.

3rd. My work is a great publicity asset for the school and my race, through the school. Had you been here last Saturday and Sunday, you would have appreciated more keenly just what that means, As I had visitors from Washington City, New York, Texas, California, etc., who kept me busy from early morning until late at night, until I was absolutely exhausted.

4th. Dozens of problems, factory and investigative are before me all of the time.

5th. Not a day passes, but what there are demands for lectures. The school wants me to go as much as possible, the reasons are obvious.

6th. I, with others, am clannish enough to want my people to receive credit for my work. I do not want my work to be swollowed up and lost the race to which I belong. Even though I, personally, may not receive a dollar of it for myself, that will come to somebody by and by.

7th. As I have intimated before, many other products are here, and are being worked out, which are interesting other factories.

8th. Now as I stated before, I have absolutely no mind for business details, all of which must be worked out satisfactory to the school and myself.

Of course you have not given any detail. You could not do so at this time. But I believe with your vision and the points which I have rather crudely and hurriedly set down that something can be worked out.

The Tom Houston Peanut Company's plan interests me more than any thing that I have come in contact with, as it is of real service to the people in general and to Southern Agriculture in particular.

This letter may not be very clear to you, but I hope you gather a sufficient amount of facts to see how complex my problem is and why I cannot do much negotiating.

With sincerely good wishes, I am

Yours very truly

G. W. Carver, Director

Agricultural Research and

Experiment Station[193]

Two years earlier, Carver had made a commitment to Tom Huston, whom he highly respected for his vision and willingness to provide oversight direction and huge financial support. Carver was certainly aware that the Tom Huston Peanut Company would also gain financially if the team's project was successful. Nevertheless, he had given his word, and because he believed he was merely an instrument of the Great Creator by whom he was allowed to develop his knowledge and his deep commitment to helping the farmers of the South, he would always help in any way he could.

In preparation for the launch of the articles about peanuts to the professional trade papers and journals, Barry wrote Carver reminding him that the date for submission of articles was the twentieth of each month. He also advised that the articles for each of the three journals should be slightly different, so that each journal published on the same topic but different content. Then Barry made the strategic suggestion that Carver expand the notice of his offer to work with each Extension agent to include the growers prior to sending it to the trade papers for publication. He ended his letter with the statement: "You sure are living up to your reputation. But I knew you would."[194]

The next two letters from Barry to Carver show the level of response to the elements of the plan and serve as indicators of progress. On June 26, 1931, Barry wrote:

Please pardon my delay in replying to your recent letters. I have just returned from the Southeastern Peanut Association convention in Panama City, Fla. I made them a talk on peanut diseases. Prof. Paul Tabor of Athens also made a short talk. Dr. Herty made a very splendid address covering the general need of cooperation and other inspirational subjects. The next time I come over to see you I want to talk things over that happened down there. Everything looks good.

Mr. Porter, Dr. Herty and myself met Dr. Miller the plant pathologist of the Univ. of Georgia, at Ft. Gaines yesterday and helped them with a disease survey. They have been out all the week and have found plenty of disease. They have also just about determined where the boundary lines of the diseased areas are. When I say they I mean also Mr. Paul Tabor and three graduate students which Dr. Miller had with him. They are going to continue this work up until harvest time, a few days at a time. How is that for getting action?

I saw Mr. Singleterry at the convention and he was very much pleased with the cooperation which you gave him on his diseased field. Dr. Miller also visited some of these fields and found 38% of the vines dead in certain tracts. Quite an eye opener.

Your letter to Dr. Taubenhaus was extremely interesting. I was especially pleased to know that he sent it to you for your approval. No doubt he will send it in in time to get it in the August issue.

I am glad that you are sending specimens to Dr. Taubenhaus also. I want all of these men to know and like you as well as I do. Cooperative work is so much more speedy.

I am glad to know that you like the specimen envelope. I only had a few envelopes on hand and had them printed up so that you could use them right away. I have ordered more and as soon as they are printed I think you will have enough to carry you for a while.

From now on things are going to pop.[195]

On July 3, he wrote:

. . . I am delighted to know that you and Mr. Higgins are getting along so well. July 4th and 5th I will spend in Atlanta and drive down to Griffin on my return trip Monday for a visit to the Ga. Experiment Station. It will be my first trip and I want to get acquainted with both the personal and the equipment. I expect to call on all of the Stations in the Southeast this Summer. Have already made a trip to the Wiregrass Experiment Station at Headland Ala. . . .

There is no danger of us giving you more credit than you deserve. We can't count that high. But you, Mr. Porter and myself will all three have to be careful that we do not cause the other workers to tire of us nor feel that there is no use of them doing anything because we have started it and will get the credit. I am trying to get as many people as possible to express themselves in writing for the magazines to overcome the danger of it appearing to be a one group proposition. I say a great deal less about you than I would like to for the above reason. So while I am not going to steal anybody else's thunder I am not going to let anybody steal yours. If necessary I can say plenty that I haven't said yet but there is a time and place to do all things. I am sure that you agree.[196]

In ongoing efforts to stay on top of anything new that might contribute to the knowledge base in support of the plan, Barry reminded Carver that:

In Dr. Taubenhaus' recent article on peanut diseases in Texas he discussed Phymatotrichum Omnivorum (root rot) but does not include the Southeastern States as a location where it is found. I thought it might be a good idea for you to ask Dr. Taubenhaus to send you a specimen so that we can all get familiar with it.[197]

Three more letters demonstrate the level of commitment to the project, the continued efforts to collect specimens to verify and strengthen the accuracy of the team's findings, the scope of the inclusion of all stakeholders, and the recognition of the hoped-for interests being raised amongst this target group. Amazingly, the collaborators with Carver in this meticulous scientific work now included botanist B. B. Higgins, who had earlier been so sharply critical.

On July 6, 1931, Carver wrote Grady Porter:

My esteemed friend Mr. Porter:

The box of peanut plants arrived in excellent condition, fresh and fine.

I have examined them microscopically, and find on two plants the typical foot rot. The spores are all immature at present, nothing but hyaline spores not divided. The plants affected with this Diplodia have that exceedingly dark bluish color, both roots and stems. We ought to be able to get the mature spores within a day of two after it rains.

I found four plants with atypical Diplodia, foot rot. I have the bulk of them planted out in moist sand to see if they develop sclerotia.

I found some fusarium on the plants affected with the Diplodia foot rot, but none on the others.

I am saving this Diplodia specimen so that you and Mr. Barry can see it when you come over.

I have just finished opening today's mail. Received a fine letter from Mr. Taubenhaus, in which he acknowledges receipt of the specimens of peanuts I sent him, and has this to say:

"The two peanut specimens which you sent me and which you marked Sclerotium rolfsii (?) were carefully examined and also placed in moist chambers. Neither of the two showed typical earmarks of Sclerotium rolfsii, and after examining today the moist chamber specimens, I found that one of them shows a typical case of Diplodia foot rot, whereas the other which could have been mistaken for Sclerotium rolfsii failed to show any growth of this fungus, but instead was over-run by rhizopus, mucor, and aspergillus.

The specimen of peanut marked Fusarium was indeed over-run by a Fusarium fungus, and it is possible that this organism caused decay or may be secondary to other things.

I am glad you are sending your Fusarium to Dr. Sherbakoff, since in my estimation he is about the best man in this country, capable and competent to pass judgement on Fusaria."

We are now getting just the kind of cooperation that will get us somewhere, just what we want.

You will note from Mr. Taubenhaus letter that he calls it Diplodia, the same as we did. He also found no Fusaria on the plants verifying the results of our examinations.

The same Diplodia foot rot will show very definitely, as will Sclerotina, the little brown shot like bodies, <u>as soon as it rains</u> [in Carver's handwriting].

It is sprinkling here a little now.

I am very proud of the specimens you sent, and I am sure we will clinch some truths.

I sent Mr. Higgins a specimen of Diplodia creberrina E. Y. E. N. Spp. on Ailanthus. I had a very cordial letter from him thanking me for it.

It is a pleasure to work with you and Mr. Barry.

I fail to find any mention of a Diplodia in Bulletin 108 [180] from Auburn. I think we will find other new things before we get through.

Just received a report from Dr. C. L. Shear on some fungi sent him. Among them was one specimen of what we choose to call Diplodia spp. Dr. Shear had identified it is Diplodia Natalensis P. Evans. on Arachis hypogea.

I am especially glad to get this determination.

Very sincerely yours,

G. W. Carver (handwritten signature [198])

On July 8, Barry wrote Carver:

Dear Dr. Carver:

Your letter of the 5th is very refreshing.

It is indeed great to know that people are really getting to work on peanut diseases. To me one of the most gratifying developments is that the other pathologists around the country are now taking you seriously and reporting on the specimens which you send in. The fact that they find the same thing that you do makes you stand out that much more.

I would like to know how you react to the articles I am writing for the three peanut trade papers every month. You will notice that the July issue carried a different article for each to avoid the uninteresting repetition. Please watch them very closely and straighten me out if I get [it] wrong anywhere.

It takes a mighty big spirit to do as much work as you have done with peanut diseases and then say you should drop in the background to give the others a chance to "Strut their Stuff." In some case this might be the right thing to do. Certainly results are more important than methods. It is my opinion that anybody who will keep the pot boiling will find out, sooner or later, who started the fire.

From left, Robert (Bob) Barry, George W. Carver, and Grady Porter, May 1931, at the Tuskegee Institute commencement presentation of the Carver Bas-Relief, a gift from Tom Huston. (Courtesy of Texas State Archives)

I saw some Ceresan[199] at Experiment Station, Ga.

Glad to learn of the pecan oil activities. The opportunities that are going to waste. Thanks for the data on Phymatotrichum.

Mr. Porter and I expect to run over to see you Friday morning.[200]

A week later, on July 15, Barry wrote Carver again:

My office man is on his vacation and I am a busy man, doing his work and mine too. But I have gotten so that I will even neglect other things to write you. So here goes.

Mr. Porter and myself also felt very much refreshed after our talk with you on the last trip. We certainly got more final data than on any previous trip.

After working a year or more on a proposition it sure is gratifying to be getting to some of the final conclusions and proofs. That, in itself, is almost reward enough. And how far we would still be away from it if it had not been for your fine [cooperation] and continual effort.

You are right in that you can see both Mr. Porter and myself understand the disease situation so much better. I am beginning to feel like I am soon going to be entitled to be called a "Path" and will then keep on trying until I can get enough information to have the "ologist" added. But, even then, I suppose there will be many who will say that I don't know anything about it. Well I guess that is one phase of peanut progress right on, so it don't hurt any.

In regard to the work of Dr. Miller, it might be too much or too far fetched. However I do not want to leave any stone unturned to get as many to work as possible and to get each to do as much as they can. The expense of Dr. Miller's first trip was financed by Washington. He was acting as Collaborator for the U.S. Dept. of Agr. Dr. Herty caused the arrangement to be made and I think he can get them to now keep Dr. Miller on it until the harvest of this Fall. The Dept. is spending much on other crops and if they will do this for peanuts I feel that nobody can get hurt by it and many might be helped. Any data that comes from the Dept. of Agr. will have more weight with the farmers. But that will not hinder our continuing as we have in the past. I am sure that you will stick with us.

Glad that you have heard from Dr. Taubenhaus again. I will be delighted to see the specimen of Phymatotrichum omnivorum on the next trip.

I am sorry that you have had no rain. Most every place has had some recently. Maybe you had better pay your preacher. But don't bring on a flood.

Yes sir, I feel good about it all too. And what give us pep to keep right after it is that we are going to feel still better about it as time goes on and control methods become better known and more generally practised.

I may not be with Mr. Porter on the next trip, on account of the various fellows taking vacations. But I will try.[201]

The preceding letter represents a critically important milestone in attaining the objectives of the plan and clearly shows the excitement generated by this realization to create momentum to continue the work by the team. Note also that the team—which had been working closely together for many months, had traveled together, had visited each other in both their work spaces and home spaces, had brought their families to visit and share meals with each other, and had pledged and shared a professional respect for each other's contributions to the successful completion of this project—showed no concerns about color. They were colorblind. They had forged an unbreakable bond, untouchable by outside negativity. This unlikely partnership of Tom and George with the addition of Barry and Porter was of four strong men who believed in themselves and what each brought to the project. Without hesitation, they offered the highest respect for each other. Together, they established a model of interracial collaboration in participatory and integrative research and disease management, a legacy which continues even stronger today.

Barry to Carver, July 20, 1931:

. . . Glad you had the rain so much needed.

Delighted to know that the County Agent at Andalusia, Ala. sent you some specimens and a letter. That's the stuff! He'll be a wiser County Agent when he gets his reply. And he will get others in the habit too.

So you found both Diplodia and Neocosmospora on the same Va. peanut vine. The plot thickens. Am I correct in that it is the first Diplodia found on any of the Va. specimens?

Fine that you are saving these specimens to show us.

Mr. Porter can tell you all about the soil in which these plants were grown and what crops they followed, and fertilizer used. Ask him about it when he comes over.

Well here is hoping I can see you again soon.

I will have a vacation about the middle of August. Do you ever get one?

Cordially yours,

TOM HUSTON PEANUT COMPANY

Bob Barry.

P.S. Mr. Porter gets a copy of all the letters I write. So he knows what goes on between you and I.

BB. [In red ink] [202]

In an interesting July 20, 1931, memorandum to Porter, copied to Carver, Barry revealed some skepticism about the peanut research going on in other states:

Grady:-

I never heard of Ghadbourn, N. C. before.

Had a letter today from the Univ. of Va., at Boyce, Va. wanting some peanuts to experiment with. I never heard of Boyce, Va. before either.

I suspicion that Va. & N.C. are getting ready to see what there is to peanut diseases, and saying as little about it as possible.

There is no telling how many people are at work on it, without our knowledge, because they are ashamed to admit how little has been done.

So things look better to me every day.

Barry [203]

Porter continued to visit farmers in Alabama, collecting samples of diseased plants and forwarding them to Carver at Tuskegee for examination. Carver responded on July 2, providing descriptive information:

My esteemed friend Mr. Porter:

The box containing the Alabama Runner, peanuts from Huston , Dale, Henry, and Barbour Counties, has arrived, been examined and found that every plant was simply covered with "Foot rot." (Diplodia natalensis P. Evans).

When you come over, I shall be interested to learn how destructive this disease was in the various counties from which these diseases come.

You are certainly getting some useful information. I am keeping all of these specimens so we can have them when needed.

Very sincerely yours

G. W. Carver [Handwritten signature] [204]

Barry wrote to Carver on July 24, telling him that Porter and he expected to come over on the following Monday morning and asking if it would be all right to bring their families, who were anxious to see Carver's headquarters.[205] In a follow-up letter, Barry told Carver that the ladies had enjoyed their visit and now understood better why he and Porter were so "Carverish." He also told Carver that he had gotten a letter from senior pathologists at the USDA saying that the department had agreed to finance another trip to the peanut belt for J. H. Miller of the University of Georgia. He should begin very soon and would "will find plenty of Sclerotium rolfsii that he hasn't found previously." [206]

So much progress had been made with the plan, and the farmers were building a strong bond with the Tom Huston Peanut Company's project. Barry wanted to ensure the company's promises were kept to provide seeds for the coming spring planting. Thus, in August, he began to plan so that an adequate supply of quality seeds was available to the farmers for the next planting season. He asked Carver for suggestions.

> I am starting this far ahead to try and determine how to get a satisfactory seed supply for next Spring and thought that you might be able to offer some very good suggestions.
>
> In the past we have kept a separate pile of farmer's stock peanuts to be cleaned up the following Spring for seed. Whenever we get in a high class lot of peanuts, unusually good, we put these in the seed pile. Then in the Spring we ran them through shakers and air lifts to take out all trash and pops. The final product was about 50% of the best part of the 100% worked.
>
> Since peanut diseases have become so marked I doubt whether this is the proper procedure to follow for the next Spring planting. It has occurred to me that we might find certain sections in Georgia that have no peanut diseases. If so we could save all of the peanuts that come into our plant from such a section and clean that up for seed. It is a question in my mind whether this would be any better. Seed produced in a disease free area and transplanted in an area that has disease in the ground might give such seed a greater shock than those produced in a diseased area and thereby not be even as satisfactory. If this is better where will we find a disease free area to collect seed from.
>
> This is just the way my mind is running and I would like to have you think it over and give me your advice.[207]

In August, Carver traveled to Fort Gaines, Georgia, and enjoyed a dinner cooked by Mrs. Porter, although Mr. Porter could not be present.

An unnamed young man drove Carver to and from Tuskegee. In the following letter of thanks, Carver updated Porter and asked him to ask the farmers some questions which would provide valuable information for future assistance:

> My dear Mr. Porter:
>
> I am so glad I made the trip, got home in ample time. Hope the boy made it back all right.
>
> I do not recall ever having seen it rain harder than it is right now. Trust you are getting some of it.
>
> Mr. Porter please note the following in going your rounds.
>
> The kinds of soil and fertilizers used.
>
> When planted.
>
> What crops they followed.
>
> Find out if peanuts were ever grown upon this land before.
>
> I believe your experiments are going to reveal just the facts we want and give us the key for improvement.
>
> I trust you are getting some rain. Please thank Mrs. Porter for me for the delicious dinner. I regret so much that you could not have shared some of it. The boy would not take any back and I have enough for my supper.
>
> Very sincerely yours,
>
> G. W. Carver [208]

Barry was glad to hear that Carver felt his trip was successful and shared updated information concerning future survey efforts:

> I was glad to have your letter of the 5th and learn that your recent trip to Ft. Gaines was interesting and profitable.
>
> In regard to the article about history repeating you can read that in the September issue of the Peanut Journal. If you happen to miss it I will be glad to supply you with a copy.
>
> Mr. Higgins has expressed a desire to go to Ft. Gaines with me next Wednesday. Mr. Funchess of Auburn has stated that he would like to go down there sometime between the 1st and 10th of August. Mr. Miller at Athens says

that he is going to start out on another survey the first of next week and make still another trip at digging time. I am trying to get them all to meet me in Columbus next Wednesday and all go to Ft. Gaines together. If they do I will certainly tell you what happens.

I enjoyed and will keep the printed slip which you sent me entitled "Aunt Jiggs Corner."

Hope to see you soon.[209]

The article Barry mentioned, entitled "Will History Repeat," was published in *The Peanut Journal*. In an earlier letter to Carver, dated August 4, 1931, Barry said he was writing an article based on information he uncovered in Farmer's Bulletin No. 302, 1907, USDA,[210] about Sea Island cotton. Barry's article would "show that the Sea Island industry has disappeared from Georgia and the peach belt has shifted, both on account of diseases." Barry intended to bring in information about the present situation on peanuts. He told Carver, "You can see from this how much room there is for a strong article based on historical facts with two other very important crops." He hoped that the publication would be advantageous to their current campaign to increase awareness of the economic impact of peanut diseases.[211]

TOM HUSTON PEANUT COMPANY REACHES OUT TO GROWERS FOR PROBLEM-SOLVING IDEAS

In a memorandum to Carver dated August 8, 1931, Barry wrote that "I have sent this [enclosed letter dated August 7, 1931] to 50 men who should have ideas about it. If they haven't any ideas it will at least make them see the necessity of getting some." The letter spoke to how farmers struggled with input costs versus output benefits and showed the need for agricultural economics as is done today in any agricultural research. In the letter to the fifty men mentioned in Barry's memorandum, he explained the purpose:

I am starting this far ahead to try and determine how to get a satisfactory peanut seed supply for next Spring. We sell about 200 tons of seed peanuts every year.

In the past we have stored every unusually good lot of peanuts that we get, in a pile to themselves. Then in the Spring we run this tonnage of farmers stock peanuts through air lifts and over screens to take out all trash and suck out all the "pops." When we get through about 50% of the best peanuts in the pile are in sacks for seed. The other 50%, which was screened out and sucked out having been shelled. Until the critical disease conditions of the last two years came along this was very satisfactory. We succeeded in putting out seed, in the hull, that analysed as follows:

	Sound & Mature Kernels	Damaged Kernels	Small Shriveled Kernels
Spring of 1930	77.33%	1.22%	1.05%
" " 1931	76.90%	1.23%	1.51%

A No. 1 peanut has 70% sound and mature kernels, about 2% damaged kernels and as few small shrivels as possible. You will notice that the seed was much better than a No. 1 and that the plantings of 1931 look about as good as 1930.

But the average germination of these seed, from many tests, in the last three seasons have run as follows:

Spring of 1929	Average germination 93.87%
" " 1930	" " 89.90%
" " 1931	" " 72.80%

So it develops that although the seed analyze very good the germination is getting worse all the time. Diseases are prevelant in the present growing crop. I would not be surprised to see seed germination, next Spring, drop below 50%, which would be a calamity.

Judging from this we will have to work out some other method of seed selection, and I would like to have your advice about how to proceed.

It might be possible to find certain areas which are disease-free. If this can be done it might be better to save all peanuts that come in from such areas instead of those that analyze the best in regard to soundness, etc. But would it? Maybe such seed, planted in diseased areas that next season would get a greater shock than seed which had matured in spite of diseases where they were produced and show an even lower % of germination.

The Georgia Experiment Station made some seed tests for us last Spring. Their figures show that the germination can be raised by dusting the seed with Ceresan or soaking them in HgCl2. But this costs money. The grower will not treat his seed. If they are treated the seller of the seed will have to do it. Then the grower will have to pay more for the seed. Even this is more or less like covering up the trouble instead of correcting it.

I will appreciate very much your full and frank advice. The seed for next Spring will have to be saved out from the crop that will start moving the latter part of next month.[212]

This memorandum is important for two reasons. First, it identifies that the plan's design to include and encourage other institutions in the research effort was working, as the Georgia Experiment Station was now participating in the project; and, second, by the selection of the fifty recipients to receive the memorandum, the three-way trust between agencies, farmers, and the Tom Huston Peanut Company had been established and was creating better understanding and sharing benefits of the unified results.

This next letter reflected a draft summary of the critical research findings that the team had been working on for the previous two years. Although the names of the fungi causing the peanut diseases are excluded, it provides preliminary suggestions for control, and suggestions for crop rotation for integrated disease management. For this reason, it might be one of the most significant letters in the collection.

My esteemed friend Mr. Barry:

Your splendid letters of August 5" and 7" have just reached me.

In your letter of August 5" you have raised one of the questions most important to peanut growers, that of satisfactory seed.

Mr. Barry, at present I think a combination of your two suggestions the best, that is:

First, make a survey of the peanut area from which you will get your seed.

Second, select fields just as free from disease as possible.

Third, use the same or similar method to those followed in the past.

Even though the ground where planted may be full of disease, the farmer has much in his favor by starting off with strong, disease free seed, which is much more likely to give him better results than if the seed and soil are both full of disease.

The severe shock of which you speak, caused by taking seed from a disease free area more or less widely separated from where they are to be planted might weaken their power of resistance, especially where there is a marked difference in the soil and climate.

I am pretty confident that at the close of this season we will be able to speak with great assurance.

The survey which I have suggested to Mr. Porter [see: letter from Carver to Porter, August 5, 1931, referenced previously], and, indeed which he has already begun, will help to clinch certain truths which are apparent already.

I went out yesterday and inspected a plot of peanuts quite one-half acre in size. The peanuts were of the Spanish variety, with a few runners mixed in here and there. I have never seen a healthier patch of peanuts. I failed to find a single diseased vine in the entire plot, every vine seemed to be the very picture of health, the vines were large and literally filled with peanuts. I did not see even any leaf spotting on the lower leaves.

These peanuts followed a corn crop, and is the first time peanuts have ever been planted on this land.

So far, control seems to point in the direction of clean seed, proper rotation of the crop and immune varieties. I will tell you more about these when I see you.

I am doing some work with peanut shells in the matter of making paper that seems most promising. I will be able to show you a sample when you come over.

Fine, I hope you can get all of those gentlemen down. I will be interested in what they find. Your article on the mole crickets is very fine.

I shall look forward to the replies from the fifty men with much interest.

Very sincerely yours,

G. W. Carver

Research and Experiment Station [213]

On August 14, 1931, Barry replied to Carver:

Thanks for your two letters of August 10th and 11th.

I have gotten a few replies from my circular to the fifty odd men about where to get peanut seed for next Spring. As soon as I get them all in I will bring them over and let you see what they had to say.

I am glad that you found a peanut field which was free from disease and that you will have some conversation about crop rotation the next time we see each other.

It is fine that you are making some paper out of peanut shells and it will be a pleasure to look your samples over when I come over.

I am glad you like the article on the mole cricket. You often refer to material which comes out in the Peanut Journal at Suffolk, Virginia. I never hear you say anything about the National Nut News of Chicago. I send them a different article every month. I have been wondering whether you get the National Nut news or not. Do you?

Dr. Miller of Athens spent last Monday in Ft. Gaines and he came to see me at the office here last Tuesday. He is making progress alright.

Yesterday Mr. Higgins of Experiment, Georgia went into the peanut fields with me and Mr. Porter and myself were able to show him plenty. While out in the fields we ran across a strange dwarfed bush of the Ala. Runner and I am sending it to you in a box, feeling sure it will interest you. I don't think I ever saw anything like it before. You will notice that it did not have any blooms, pegs or peanuts on it and seems to have a tendency to be affected with some kind of Rosette.

In the same box is a cotton stalk which will show some Ozonium, I think. This cotton stalk was against the root of this dwarfed peanut vine.

I am delighted to know that you will help me work out a dinner with peanut products. I am enclosing a little rough menu which is on my mind that might guide you some in making your selection.

I start out on a vacation next Saturday and will be gone for two weeks. I will be at the Signal Mountain Hotel at Signal Mountain, Tenn., just out from Chattanooga and will be glad to hear from you up there if you are not too much loaded up.[214]

Attached to Barry's preceding August 14, 1931, letter to Carver was the memo at right. Barry had previously mentioned "teaching his wife how to prepare a complete meal with peanuts alone, if possible, so that I can serve it to any company I might have from time to time. I think it would be good peanut advertising."[276] Carver then replied to Barry with the below page 2 of his letter commenting on the notion.

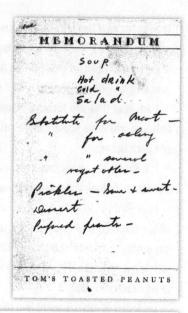

chocolate-coated ect, etc. Also the time honored vender with his little bags of fresh perched peanuts, with which we are all familiar.

As I thought of the 150 or more ways into which the peanut can be prepared for human consumption alone, I marveled at the fact that not a single person was there demonstrating some of the many many attractive and appetizing ways in which they can be served. What could be more attractive, simple and nourishing than a fine course luncheon similiar to the following:

1. (Peanut soup, served
   (with peanut wafers
   (This luncheon may be varied according to taste.

2. (Peanut biscuit, mock chicken
   (or meat loaf
   (peanut oleo.

3. (Peanut-butter sandwiches
   (made with the peanut wafers,
)peanut salad.

4. (Peanut custard
   (or
   (mince pie.

5. (Peanut ice cream
   (served with
   (peanut cake

6. (Black coffee with salted peanuts
   (and whatever kind of peanut candies
   (one wishes.

This menu has been served to a large number of very fastidious people and without exception, each and all said that it was the most satisfying luncheon they had ever eaten. You will note with interest that no meat has been included in the menus.

I believe that if even one-half of the time, energy, etc, were put forth in advertising the peanut that is put upon many of the things we have above mentioned, we would not only double peanut consumption but perform a distinct and beneficial service to humanity.

A PIVOTAL MOMENT OCCURS as this point in the Plan! Finally! An indication of the USDA's recognition of the disease problem and the willingness to provide financial support for confirmation of the cause! As part of the plan's continuing education outreach effort, Barry sent Carver a copy of an open letter he was sending to growers explaining the disease problem, Dr. Miller's role and visit, and directions for site preparation as a way to help themselves prepare for next spring's crop:

Dear Sir:

Some growers know it and some do not. But PEANUT DISEASES have been cutting down their profit. The DISEASES lower the yield per acre. They also cause a poor grade that lowers the value of the peanuts.

This company has spent a great deal of time and money to work out methods of DISEASE CONTROL, for the PEANUT GROWERS. The U. S. Department of Agriculture at Washington is paying the expenses for Dr. Miller of Athens, Ga., to make three trips into the PEANUT BELT and study the PEANUT DISEASES. He is also doing a great deal of Laboratory work. In time Dr. Miller and others will be able to tell what to do about it.

But in the meantime you can be doing something for yourself. I would suggest that you spend considerable time in your peanut fields right now. Stake off a great many PEANUT VINES that look better, and have more peanuts on them, than the others. As soon as these staked off peanuts are mature, dig them with a mattock[215] and examine the roots and peanuts on them. If there is no sign of MOULD OR ROT on them, and if the pegs holding the peanuts on the vine are strong and solid, put them in stacks to themselves. This means that those vines have resisted the DISEASES better than the others. If you will plant these for seed next Spring, your crop will be more resistant to the DISEASES, next year. If you will do this every year you will, in time, go a long way towards developing a strain of seed that will not be damaged by disease. When you have completely accomplished this you can get a Patent from the U. S. Government to protect you for your work. YOU COULD SELL SUCH SEED TO OTHERS AT A VERY FANCY PRICE.

Enclosed you will find some literature on the MOLE CRICKET,[216] which damages the peanut crop. If you will poison him you will get more and better peanuts per acre.

We have enlarged our wagon and truck scale. It is now 26 feet long and should weigh any truck that comes in. Have also made better arrangements for unloading trucks that will save them time.

WE EXPECT TO BUY YOUR PEANUTS THIS FALL, the same as usual. Don't forget us.

Cordially yours,

TOM HUSTON PEANUT COMPANY

Bob Barry, Mgr.

Shelling Dept. [217]

Activities really began hopping now! As the interest in the peanut industry grew and the recruitment of new growers expanded, the need for larger storage space became evident at the Tom Huston Peanut Company. To meet this demand, the Shelling Department, which had just started shelling the new crop, began the construction of a new building. Its storage capacity would be four thousand tons of farmer's stock peanuts, and it had to be completed within thirty days! The harvesting of the experimental plots at Fort Gaines, Georgia, was in progress, and many growers were asking for information as they made their plans to move their crops.[218]

More good news came to Carver from Barry when he wrote that, "Mr. Moore, one of the associate pathologists of the Bureau of Plant Industry, has been in the peanut belt all this week and I am expecting him in my office this afternoon. He has been dumbfounded by the disease situation of peanuts in the South and his report to Washington will no doubt cause the explosion which we have all expected to happen sooner or later."[219]

Barry also forwarded a copy of a letter from E. C Mann, an Extension agent in Georgia, for the purpose of showing Carver that "some of the Georgia county agents are becoming interested enough to get out and look things over. The work which you so graciously helped us get started, or did we help you, is certainly showing a high percent of germination."[220]

Barry again wrote to Carver that he had recently found out about the *Plant Disease Reporter*, a monthly or sometimes semi-monthly publication of the Bureau of Plant Industry at Washington; he asked for copies to be sent to himself, Carver, and Porter. He alerted Carver that he had a request from the local county agent for distribution of some graphic information to acquaint the farmers with the grades of peanuts and how grading was used. [See Appendix A] The agent also asked for an exhibit at the Chattahoochee Valley Fair on the control of peanut diseases. Barry asked Carver for assistance in putting together a display of materials that would show not only the importance of disease control but would also let attendees know what was being done about this issue.[221]

Barry updated Carver on information about the *Plant Diseases Reporter* that he obtained from Dr. Miller. He said he was sure that they would all benefit from the information:

> . . . I do not know who is supposed to furnish material for this reporter but imagine it is the baby of the U. S. Department of Agriculture. It would be very interesting to see what they would do with report from a man like you, who is not with the Department of Agriculture. I am wondering if you wouldn't like to try that out . . . [222]

The work was gathering momentum and much-needed, and hoped for, recognition and support. In the next letter to Carver, Barry reported more exciting news: that interest in peanut diseases is growing among federal researchers.

> I am glad to have your letter of the 15th.
> I sent a copy of the market news letter to Dr. Herty in New York and he turned it over to Dr. Woods at the U.S. Dept. of Agriculture, Washington, requesting that he make an investigation in the Virginia North Carolina section, which is very much closer to Washington than Georgia is. I hope something comes of it but the Department of Agriculture is so short of funds it is practically impossible for them to do the things that they know they do.
> I haven't been very busy at the Fair but the new crop of peanuts is now moving and this keeps me from devoting any time or thought to anything else for the time being. With this whole end of town full of trucks and farmers, of necessity other things have to wait but I will be back on the disease situation with both feet just as soon as I can possibly concentrate on it.
> How are you feeling now?[223]

The momentum continued, as Barry wrote Carver to apprise him of the actions taken since Dr. Herty asked Dr. Woods to investigate the peanut situation in Virginia and North Carolina.

I was glad to hear from you again on the 22nd.

I am glad to be able to report that Dr. Moore who we talked to you about, has just written me a letter stating that Dr. Stevens at Washington has sent a man down into the Virginia North Carolina peanut territory to check up on the root rot which was reported in the recent market letter which I sent you. I suppose his findings will be a deep dark secret though for the rest of time. Dr. Woods also stated that Washington was very much interested in the report he made about the Southeastern Peanut Belt. Of course if the Department of Agriculture had sufficient funds I think we could expect big things of them, but they haven't. the necessary money to do what they would even like to do.

I am always interested in reports of activities over at Tuskegee and only hope that you will not tackle more than you can stand. I wouldn't call you an old man without expecting to get a bump on my head but you are older than you once were you know and will have to be careful of over doing.[224]

The peanut harvesting season was now in full swing. The expanded number of growers committed to the Tom Huston Peanut Company were bringing in their peanuts, and Barry wrote Carver of the level of increased traffic coming into the plant:

Your letters of the 24th and 26th were welcome as usual. Please pardon me if I do not reply to them as soon as I would like. We are all loaded to the breaking point now with the movement of the new crop. About 200 tons per day are now coming into our plant and most of it is by truck so the whole plant is full of truck drivers and farmers trying to sell peanuts . . .

Mr. Porter is very much alive. He is dashing all over the peanut belt now trying to help me keep posted on market conditions and the movement of the crop.

Dr. Herty was here day before yesterday and he will keep right in behind Washington on all of these disease matters . . . [225]

Barry wrote to Carver early in November 1931 to let him know that "Dr. Herty was in the office just a short while last week and is still working on Washington. I think in the course of time he will get them to put out a little money on peanut diseases. It is hard to make anybody spend these days. It is interesting to know that you have found diplodia Natalensis [sic] on the sycamore tree. Isn't it remarkable how information will go." [226]

Carver was surprised when Porter wrote that he had moved his family to Columbus, Georgia, and will now be working in the Huston plant. His duties included handling all the farmers coming into the plant so he would the opportunity to talk about peanut diseases and the food value of the peanut. He used Carver's recipes and his reports to share with both "white and colored" farmers. He hoped they would not only try the recipes but also share them with neighbors. [227]

Because of Porter's agricultural skills and knowledge, as well as his ability to convey his respect of the farmers and their efforts, he had provided the strongest possible link between the Tom Huston Peanut Company and the growers. He had certainly delivered on his assigned responsibility as part of the plan. And, because of events swirling outside the purview of the team and its charge which would affect the future of Tom Huston Peanut Company, assigning Porter to the new role would prove to be an excellent management decision.

The team's work was progressing rapidly, with the final details and results being added on a daily basis. The realization that success was close created much excitement during the next few months.

6

It All Comes Together, or Mission Accomplished

"Tom was the darling of the farmers who now had a ready market for their peanuts. The company was teaching them better farming methods to get more yield and better quality crops."
—*Candy*[228]

B ecause of the careful planning and hours spent putting the plan into action, its elements were coming to fruition. After two years of research and awareness building, targeted people were now involved; the culture of peanut processing and the thinking of industry decision-makers were changing. In a mid-December 1931 letter to Carver, Bob Barry celebrated an early Christmas gift for the team:

> No doubt you have received your peanut Plant Reporter of Dec. 15th 1931 and discovered that the whole eleven pages is devoted to peanut diseases.
> When I got my copy I had to shake hands with myself in the mirror and feel that you, after so much work, will want to do the same thing. As for me I am going to make a special trip over to Tuskegee just to do some handshaking with you about it.
> To me this report is the crowning point of all the work we have done for the last two years . . . It shows that peanut diseases are a very serious handicap to the whole peanut industry over a number of different States and the fact that is has come from what is considered the highest authority, on the subject, in the whole nation, puts the matter now to where not even a congressman can afford to overlook it and do nothing about alleviating the damage to a fifty million dollar crop.

> Dr. Herty is now working on a good many congressmen from the peanut States in an effort to get an appropriation to extend this work on into a study of methods of control. This report has come out just in time to be used in the new session of Congress and I am very much delighted over the whole proposition. I know you are.
>
> Won't Grady Porter be tickled when he finds it out?[229]

In the coming days, Barry continued to share his excitement, as well as his concern. He wrote Carver again on December 23:

> ... The more I think of the Peanut Disease acknowledgement by the Bureau of Plant Industry the better I feel. Of course, like you, I cannot agree with them 100% but if it was 50% wrong the fact that they are now convinced that disease is really very damaging to the fifty million dollar peanut crop, it is something to have accomplished. If you hadn't had the courage, and it took plenty of that, to publish your bulletin, peanut damage would still just be "damaged peanuts."
>
> Mr. Porter and myself both enjoyed our last visit to you. But this is always the case. Did you ever stop to think how many new things have developed on these numerous visits. That convinces me that we are working with the right man.
>
> Sincerely hope that you have a fine Christmas. I have sent you a box of candy but won't ask whether you ate it or not. I know you.[230]

In March 1932, Barry sent Carver a copy of a report, "Disease Control Experiments with Peanuts, February 1932 by Bob Barry and Grady Porter, Tom Huston Peanut Company, Columbus, GA.," which he had sent to the officials of the Tom Huston Peanut Company providing the results of the field work conducted during the 1931 growing season. Barry included his own thoughts and asked for Carver's comments and constructive criticisms:

> ... It seems evident that the best and quickest way out of peanut field difficulties is for the Dept. of Agriculture to develop a disease resisting strain to be used for seed, such as has been done with other crops.
>
> The Dept. of Agriculture has the men with the necessary training and possibly all the equipment needed for such work. But no money is available for

it. Everybody interested in the welfare of the Peanut Industry should make an effort to get an appropriation through the present session of Congress to aid this fifty million dollar crop.[231]

The opening paragraph of the report stated:

In the 1930 growing season we saw a great deal of damage to the peanut crop from plant diseases. A study of the situation was carried on throughout the season. We also made and [*sic*] earnest effort to locate anyone who had experience with control methods but did not find anybody who was working it out. Although we knew that we were not sufficiently trained along this line, something had to be done, and, in addition to about 20 acres of peanuts planted for general cultural work, we cut up 1¾ acres to be used for a try at disease control.

A map of this work is attached with figures inserted to show the outcome of the venture. Every line on the map represents a row of peanuts. You will notice that we had 39 rows planted to Small Spanish, 39 to Virginia Bunch and 39 to Virginia Runners. Each 39 rows represents 13 tests, 3 rows to the test. Each row was 130 feet long. All peanuts that were pulled up for observation throughout the season were taken from the north 30 feet of each row. The harvested rows were all the same length, 100 feet long.[232]

The fifteen-page report provided extensive data from the entire year of experimental efforts and results. Explanations of fertilization times, amounts, compounds, grades and yield at harvest for each of the three types of peanuts planted are shown. Detailed discussion was provided for any problems encountered. An extensive section described the diseases encountered and identified each disease. This was followed by a section of Field Notes by month and date, from April 21 through October 16, 1931. The last page of the report presented a chart of the cost of the three-row disease control work: $184.57, including seed, fertilizer, land, labor, equipment, supervision, etc., and credits given for peanuts shipped/pound: $14.63, with the experiment's total cost of $169.94.

On page 9 of the report, Barry and Porter made their summary statement.

Last summer Dr. Julian H. Miller was appointed Collaborator for the U.S. Dept. of Agriculture to work with peanuts. His expenses were paid but I am of the opinion that he received no salary for his summer work. He teaches at the University of Georgia in the winter. We are of the opinion that Dr. Miller has already accomplished a great deal.

The Plant Disease Reporter of December 15, 1931, shows the results of a peanut disease survey conducted by the Bureau of Plant Industry. The seriousness of the situation is evident in it.

We have spent a great deal of time and money making a study of peanut diseases and interesting others in it. It seems that everybody is now convinced that it is a serious proposition and that much work needs to be done on it quickly. Hence we have accomplished our purpose and now feel that we should be allowed to discontinue any further work in the field along this line. It is the job of men who are much more highly trained to it than we are and who have the U.S. Dept. of Agriculture behind them. We would like to help in any way that we can. An appropriation of only $5,000.00 would be sufficient to carry this work through another summer. It will not do all that should be done but will keep the work going until better conditions make it possible to get more appropriation. I sincerely hope that all concerned will make some effort to get this appropriation through the present session of Congress. This fifty million dollar crop has been neglected too long already. Some very interesting work has been done with peanuts but none seems to have been directed at disease control.[233]

The report was critical because it was the showpiece for the entire plan envisioned by Tom Huston and represented the long, long hours of planning, research, and hard work by Barry, Porter, and Carver for the previous four years. The report published, for the first time, data identifying peanut diseases, correlating that data with field-work descriptions of diseased plants and the design of experimental fertilization/treatment plots. Also, the lessons learned from the experimental work were shared with farmers for use in their own fields.

This was a huge accomplishment for both the farmers and the industry. It also represented the formal completion of the plan. Now the responsibility for survival of the peanut industry would rest upon the the federal level.

The Tom Huston Peanut Company had done the research groundwork by supporting the development, design, implementation, and extensive data collection documenting the problems affecting the survival of the peanut industry. Although the work and data collection would continue at the company, the focus now would be on crop improvement and continued work directly with the growers, while continuing to share findings with the researchers, Extension agents, and elected officials. Barry continued to attend meetings and share information. Carver continued to entertain visitors from the highest levels of USDA.

In an April 25, 1932, letter to Carver, Barry wrote:

I enjoyed your letter of the 20th and glad to know that the two pathologists from Washington came over to see you. I believe that this is the most co-operative stroke that they have made towards you yet, isn't it?

Dr. Paul Miller will be at Tifton, Georgia for several months studying peanut diseases, I understand. There is both a shelling plant and an Experiment Station there. The only place of that kind in the Georgia Peanut Belt.

He will find something. Won't he?[234]

On the following day, Barry wrote again to Carver:

I am very glad to learn from your letter of the 23rd that you found the two pathologists from Washington very alive and raring to go.

As soon as I can find your menu made of peanut products I want to work up what I will call a Peanut Party. I would like to have the menu printed on paper made from peanut hulls and have been wondering whether you could supply this thin enough.

Mr. Porter was in the office yesterday and said he was getting up a few things to take over which he thinks you will be interested in. One thing he wants to take up is specimens to show you the deterioration of Austrian peas in the few years in which they have been planted out of their natural habitat[235]

In May, Carver received a cordial, handwritten letter from Dr. Paul Miller of the Mycology and Disease Survey in the USDA Bureau of Plant Industry:

This is to acknowledge your kind letter of April 30.

I can assure you our visit with you was greatly enjoyed and your hospitality much appreciated. I shall remember it with much pleasure, and if you get up to Washington D.C. I want to be sure and see you.

I would appreciate having specimens of any of the rusts sent to me at the Washington office.

I am finding some Fusarium spp and Bacterial trouble on the peanut seedlings.

If there is any way that I can be of service to you, let me know.

Thanking you again for the kindness.[236]

Miller's visit was an honor for Carver. The two scientists would correspond, visit, and share samples until Carver's death.

In June, Barry wrote to Carver with a question:

I remember that on the first trip we made to your office you said that you had seen diseases on peanuts, at the Experiment Farm there, and had reported it to Washington, with no reply.

[It] would be interesting to know just what year that was. It would give some inkling of how long the diseases have been developing unmolested.

Would you mind telling me?

For economical reasons it looked like I was going to lose Mr. Porter, for awhile. But he is still on the job., I am very glad to say, and I hope I can swing on to him forever.

How are you feeling these days?[237]

Barry wrote again four days later.

I appreciate very much your letter of June 1st and 3rd.

Save all the questions you care to. I will be glad to answer them as best I can.

It is very very interesting to know that you saw peanut plants affected by diseases way back in 1903. This shows that they have existed for at least 29 years. Nobody knows how much longer. No doubt Washington did not show much interest at that time because peanuts had not become a large commercial crop in this section of the country then. The first shelling plant was built at Edison, Georgia in 1916 or 1917.[238]

While preparing to attend the 1932 Southeastern Peanut Association's convention in Florida, Barry told Carver that he would be presenting information on peanut diseases. And, because he knew Carver had a special interest in hybridization, he went on:

> . . . While I am at Panama City, attending the convention, I am going to try and run on down to Gainesville, Florida to visit the Experiment Station there. They have invited me a number of times and have some very interesting stuff that I would like to see. One thing in particular is a cross between the Virginia Bunch and the Small White Spanish in the fifth generation. They are trying to produce a peanut which will suit Southeastern conditions, but a large size, so that our Southeastern money does not have to go to Virginia and North Carolina for the large podded types.
>
> I have just finished making my notes for the peanut disease address at the convention and was somewhat surprised to find out how much there really was to say. It is difficult to realize the extent of the progress until it is all laid out on paper for several years in its right sequence. And what I am telling you is that if you had not taken in two plant disease novices and made it possible for us to talk turkey to the technical men the matter would have been a dead issue two years ago. Now watch your step. When I do turn a spanking aloose it is a spanking.[239]

In a follow-up to his Florida trip, Barry told Carver:

> ". . . The Experiment Station . . . has some very wonderful stuff which I have never seen before and I wouldn't take a thousand dollars for my trip down there.
> . . . I will be delighted to talk to you about a method of crossing peanuts which you suggest might give us what we want. I would like to do a little work of that kind and I never have . . ."[240]

Still receiving positive comments from his Florida trip, Barry congratulated Carver for receiving a letter from the Southeastern Peanut Association:

. . . They all wanted to know how Grady and I found out so much about plant diseases and we simply told them the truth as it is.[241] Neither Mr. Porter nor myself made a motion for the resolution[242] nor seconded it nor had anything else to do with it except vote for it. The rest of the fellows were only too glad to do it. Really there was a very unusual amount of enthusiasm in regard to it, which of course was very pleasing to Mr. Porter and myself.[243][244]

Normally, in a successful business model, as one phase of the business plan ends and is evaluated, the next phase of the plan began. And so it

An unusual hand-made card mailed by Barry to Carver in 1932 was testimony to the relationship the two men enjoyed.

happened at the Tom Huston Peanut Company. Just not in the way one might expect—based on the successful results achieved by the efforts of the team. Sadly, during the next months, major changes were happening at the highest level within the Tom Huston Peanut Company that spelled the beginning of its end as we have come to know it. In June 1932, a small red flag went up, as noted in a letter from Barry to Carver. Barry commented, "For economical reasons it looked like I was going to lose Mr. Porter, for awhile. But he is still on the job, I am very glad to say, and I hope I can swing on to him forever."[245]

In September, Barry wrote Carver twice to share some of these changes:

I enjoyed both your letter of the 13th and the 15th.

The information you gave about chestnut disease is very interesting and I hate to see the fine old trees disappear.

My superintendent has left me now and I am playing both manager and superintendent and general flunkey. Mr. Porter is here helping me temporarily and may have to stay here. I regret very much to say that it does not look like we will be able to see you much this Winter. The program of economy now underway will prohibit us from doing a great many things that we would like to do but cannot. Anyhow think of us as much as you can and drop me a line once in a while and let me know how you are getting along. We all appreciate your help and friendship very much and want to keep in touch with you as closely as possible to do under existing conditions.[246]

The second letter, two days later, read:

I was very glad to get your two letters of the 19th and it is good to know that you liked my address on peanut diseases.

We now have in our office a petition to the next Congress for Federal Aid in working out peanut disease troubles. We will get every peanut grower that comes into our plant to sign this if he will. All of the other shellers said that they would do the same thing and if they will possibly our Southeastern congressmen will get the names of 10 or 15 thousand growers asking for this same thing. I don't see how they can afford to overlook that. Do you?

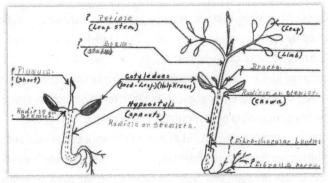

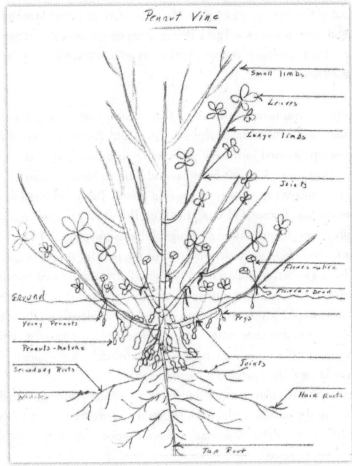

Drawings to help Barry prepare the displays for the "little museum" in the lobby of the Huston Peanut Company.

It is interesting to know that you recently found two diseases, heretofore unobserved by us, and I would like to take alook at them the next time I am over there if I ever find time to get there again.

I recently had a letter from Dr. Sherbakoff saying that he found Colletatrichum (anthranose) on some recent specimens. In his letter he did not say anything about finding gloesporium or phyllosticta or vermicularia.

The company wants me to cut out as much field work as possible and instead of hiring another superintendent and jeopardizing Mr. Porter's position I now have him in the plant and expect to make a shelling plant superintendent out of him. For this reason he will be pretty much tied down here and I doubt if either one of us will get a chance to run over to see you anything like as often as we have in the past. As much as we hate that it seems to be necessary now.[247]

Despite these apparent restrictions that accompanied changes at the management level, the team carried on. Barry and Porter completed the "little museum" located inside the plant lobby, containing glass cases set in wood stained using Carver's formulas and built to his specifications, in which they displayed specimens of diseased plants. Barry mounted other specimens in glass frames and hung them on the walls. He also prepared botanically correct identification drawings of the peanut plant, for which he asked for Carver's help with identification of the parts in simple language for the farmers to better understand.[248] He and Porter anticipated opening the museum to the entire peanut industry and expected that 90 percent of the visitors would be peanut growers. They also completed an exhibit for the October Chattahoochee State Fair and were extremely pleased with the interest shown by the attending farmers. They provided microscopes so the farmers could view the diseases for themselves.[249]

In developing the plan, one objective was to include women, especially farm wives, in the outreach education efforts. In a letter to Carver, M. M. Osborn, editor of *The Peanut Journal*, a major supporter during the public relations blitz, suggested:

Dear Friend:

I have been thinking of a service that you thru The Peanut Journal can do the shellers and cleaners in matter of them increasing their sales.

That is to bring the attention to the one thing they are neglecting that of increasing the use of Peanuts in every household. You know at present that very few of the grocery stores over the country are handling peanuts on sale.

Also the 5 and 10 cent stores are neglected. I noticed recently that some one in Norfolk (Va.) are selling roasted peanuts giving the purchaser much more for a nickle and they are doing pretty good business. The idea is to get the shellers to have their salesmen in their territory call other stores and get them to sell peanuts either roasted or raw, giving them four or five ounces for 5¢ or sell them at say 15¢ a pound. Impress on them to keep them absolutely fresh then they will come back often . . .

. . . Write it up, if you will and don't be Stingy about using our space as we are here for that purpose. Best of luck to you. Hope you are having good health . . .

Yours very truly,

M. M. Osborn

Peanut Journal Publishing Co.[250]

Osborn wrote again in August.

Excuse the delay but I have just read your letter of June 22. We published your article in August issue. In this letter you mentioned a matter that I feel of great importance to the readers now and that is this "I had in mind the organization of those interested in marketing Peanuts so that they would make a united and continuous effort until the Peanut appeared in every home, restaurant, café, and eating house as an essential part of the daily meal, or menu, the same as potatoes, peas, etc."

Do you think you have time to prepare me a thorough [story] on this subject? If so remember that I will appreciate this great lift and it will be of great help to the peanut trade. They want such things to help them in putting over the story to the housewife.

Write it up completing the excellent food value of Peanuts, etc., and let us
have same as soon as you get it together.

You know we always appreciate all other stories you have furnished us and
feel under great obligations to you. Let us hear from you soon.

Yours very truly,

M. M. Osborn [Hand signed][251]

On August 24, 1932, Carver sent Osborn a nine-page article, "Creative
Thought and Action, One of the Greatest Needs of the South."[252]

It is interesting that Osborn did not tell the brand of the five-cent
peanuts that he described in his first letter. It suggests that the brand was
not a Tom Huston's product, since Osborn had been publishing Huston's
ads for years; or perhaps he was simply unaware of the marketing method
used by Huston. It is also possible that the Tom Huston Peanut Company
was not placing salesmen in the Suffolk, Virginia, area, home of *The Peanut
Journal* Publishing Company at this time. It certainly seems that the plan
Osborn was suggesting was the very sales model that Tom Huston Peanut
Company was founded upon. It is also interesting that in August 1932, Barry
informed Carver that "he and his family will be leaving on an auto trip to
the mountains of N. C. and will run up into the Va. peanut belt before I
return . . . It is supposed to be a vacation."[253] Perhaps this was an omen of
changes to come.

One of the ways selected to increase the in-home use of peanuts was to
begin adding recipes and demonstrations to presentations and publications.
An October 1932 letter from Barry to Carver spoke to that effort:

. . . I am very glad you liked our ad in last Sunday's Ledger [perhaps referring
to the *Columbus Ledger Inquirer*] in an effort to put peanuts into the homes.
In this connection what do you now think of the various grades of chopped
peanuts which we supplied you to use with various receipts [recipes]. Is this
the product that the public would need to make better use of them at home? If
you think so would we be safe to go ahead and put out a product of that kind
on a small scale for a try-out? . . . [254]

Two months earlier, Carver had requested some granulated peanuts to
see if they would produce a product that would not stick to the top of the

mouth like regular peanut butter. In response, Barry sent Carver three jars of peanut butter; one labeled Huston's regular product, one coarse ground, and one medium-coarse ground. He asked for Carver's opinion as well as suggestions for improvement.[255] In mid August, Barry wrote Carver:

> I am sorry that we did not get over to see you as I wrote we might. Things are happening so fast over here that plans will not work out. The peanut market is now very active and the price has risen a full cent a pound for Shelled No. 1's. This requires a great deal of work to keep posted. I am due a vacation for 10 days but it looks like it is too late to get away. If I do go or do not I will try to see you first.
>
> In addition to the three grindings of Peanut Butter I sent you 4 jars of chopped peanuts which I think will serve your purpose better than the butter. You will notice that the oil did not escape. The two grades all came out of the chopper together. We sifted the fine particles out of the coarse to get the two grades. Two jars were cooked peanuts and two raw, except for the light roast necessary to blanch them.
>
> You will be interested to know that I have a car now moving from a Ga. point, loaded with Va. Peanuts raised in Ga., which I will shell here. There is a possibility of getting as much as 250 tons more of it from the same section when harvested. It is better than anything I have seen from Va. I found all of the diseases in the growing crop, down there, but it was very hard to find, hence not so serious. I was surprised to find how well posted they [sic] growers in that section were on the presence of diseases in Ga. peanuts. It shows how far reaching our agitation has been . . .
>
> As ever,
> Barry[256]

In October 1932, Grady Porter wrote Carver about a recent visit:

> Thank you very much for your letter with reference to my visit to you and Dr. Miller. I am glad that he had the chance to go back to see you on his way north.
>
> I sent you some specimens yesterday. These were taken from the same field from which I sent you specimens on or about September 2nd. I have a letter

from Dr. C. D. Sherbakoff stating that he found Colletatrichum (anthracnose) and I wanted you to be on the look out for the same thing in case you had not found it.[257]

On the bottom of that letter, Carver handwrote "Colletatrichum Vermicularia 9-17-1932."

CORRESPONDENCE BETWEEN THE TEAM members continued as usual, progress continued to be made, and successes continued to be shared. Barry wrote Carver twice in late October, first on the 24th:

Your letter of the 21st, announcing the discovery of another peanut disease, is very interesting and if possible I would like to have you send me a specimen and give me some idea about how to locate it with the naked eye. Mr. Porter has returned my microscope and it would give me great pleasure to take a look at it and seek the things which you have sketched on your letter . . .[258]

And again on the 26th to Carver's interim reply:

I enjoyed your letter of the 23rd very much and am glad to know that your article will appear in the next issue of the Peanut Journal.

I don't know yet what will become of the chopped peanut idea. From my present position I couldn't put it over unless it was acceptable to some of the others . . .

. . . I presume you read the report of Paul Miller in the October 15th Plant Disease Reporter on the results of his trip to the peanut belts in April, May, August and Sept. of this year. I consider his report too brief but believe it is on account of holding the expense down on all Government publications.[259]

Among the letters in the Carver files, the following seems at first to be somewhat out of place. Although from Tom Huston to Carver, it is not on the usual Tom Huston Peanut Company letterhead. In fact, a small return address at the top left corner stated only: "Tom Huston, Columbus, Georgia." Its stark simplicity seemed to announce the end of the beloved company that

Huston had founded in 1925 and forced the reader to accept that he was no longer part of the organization. Although his name would remain on the building and the official letterhead, Huston had been replaced by Walter Richards, formerly the vice president. The letter, sadly, may be understood as a farewell letter to a faithful friend, paying tribute for the shared vision during the years of this pioneering journey, almost from its beginning:

> Dear Dr. Carver:
>
> While a little slow in saying so I must congratulate you on your very wonderful and interesting write-up which recently appeared in the American Magazine. You certainly deserve a place on America's front page. The American Magazine is just that for those who have accomplished things.
>
> You have my sincere good wishes for continued good health that will enable you to continue your good work.
>
> Sincerely,
>
> [Hand-signed signature]
>
> Tom Huston
>
> TH:R
>
> November 15, 1932[260]

Despite the undoubtedly difficult organizational changes taking place within the Tom Huston Peanut Company, the Barry-Porter-Carver team continued with its plan of work and observed increases in results. By this time, the team, with other supportive colleagues, including researchers, had published approximately forty peanut-related articles in the three selected trade publications. Their content had broadened the understanding of the challenges unique to each season of the year and had provided peanut growers with invaluable technical assistance. Barry and Carver continued to discuss the feedback from their efforts. On December 20, 1932, Barry wrote Carver:

> I was very glad to get your letter of the 15th.
>
> I wrote the article on the Nutritive Value of Peanuts at the request of one of our present officials and they tell me they expect to use it in some way or

another to boost sales. It will possibly be cut up and used a little bit at a time. If it is published I will be glad to send you a copy of it.

I was very much interested in your statement that there is always a something that encourages me to push ahead.

The motto of the Barry coat of arms is -"Boutez en Avant" which means press forward. I have always felt that I was living up to it mighty poorly so your remark was full of inspiration as usual.[261]

BY 1933, LETTERS BECAME noticeably fewer and fewer among the team members. This was due, no doubt, to the impact of the ownership changes at the Tom Huston Peanut Company. But there was also the tremendously satisfying knowledge that, while the interests in peanut diseases and quality of peanut crops is certainly not waning, the responsibility and research oversight efforts had been bumped up to the scientists at the federal level.

Carver, however, continued his vast correspondence and was in touch regularly with Drs. Paul Miller, L. L. Shear, and C. D. Sherbakoff, sharing both specimens and the data generated amongst themselves and others. A handwritten letter from Miller, written in February 1934 while on an assignment in Knoxville, Tennessee, illustrates the esteem in which Carver was held by his contemporaries.

Dear Dr. Carver:

I can think of no more appropriate day than this, to write you, the birthday of the great man [a reference to Abraham Lincoln] who made it possible for you, my esteemed and admirable friend, to enjoy doing a worthwhile service to your race and to the people in general of the United States.

I have been very busy since arriving in Knoxville, but I can say I have found the survey to be extremely interesting, and it seems to fit in well with the plans of the "New Deal" in general and with the Tennessee Valley Authority, specifically. A body of data is gradually accumulating which I believe will be significant to those interested in agricultural advancement.

I am wondering how you are getting along with your fungi, chemical experiments and studies with the oils. Have you considered your Botany textbook lately?

If you perchance find any more "good" rusts, I would appreciate receiving them at the Agr. Exp. Sta, University of Tenn., Knoxville, Tenn., as I will probably be here for some time.

Dr. Carver, I wonder if you might have a photograph of yourself that you would send me?

Have you heard from our friend, Bob Barry recently?

Well, Dr. Carver, as I have told you several times before, I think you are doing a great piece of work, and I am truly thankful that I have had the opportunity of knowing you.

I shall be glad to hear of all your activities the past few months,

With Kindest and Sincere Regards,

Paul R. Miller[262]

In another handwritten letter, on hotel stationery, dated May 29, 1934, Bob Barry surprised Carver with the information that he had moved his family to Greensboro, North Carolina and was traveling across that state, Virginia, Maryland, and parts of West Virginia and South Carolina, as district sales manager for the Tom Huston Peanut Co. He said he had "managed to increase sales 20 percent so far. But it is quite a job." Barry asked Carver to write "for I will always consider you one of my very best friends." He added a note: "Do you suppose you could figure out a way to freshen stale candy? We have to pick up quite a bit of it from stores and this is quite a loss."[263]

The team's friendships would continue for a lifetime. Their plan had been accomplished with phenomenal success. The work was even more important as the industry continued to grow, and the research was still ongoing. But it was now at the highest level where it could benefit the most people.

7

Tom and George, after the Peanut Company

Tom was a Seeker but not a Finder. He was forever reach-
ing for a nebulous goal that constantly eluded him. He was
a sower of seeds who never stayed around for the harvest. His
restless mind the tool of his talents never found a resting place.
It was his glory and his defeat.

—From a document by an unknown author in
the archives of Columbus State University[264]

A short five years after its beginning in 1925, the founder of the Tom Huston Peanut Company began to look for new ways to channel his creativity. Huston explained it this way in an account he later wrote:

> In March, 1930, my sun was shining brightly. Five years previously I had en-
> tered the field of merchandising peanuts. The starting place was a one-story
> shack. In those five short years my shack grew into a modern daylight factory,
> over 600 feet in length. With annual sales running into the millions, and net
> earnings more than a quarter of a million each year, the desire to conquer new
> fields was running in my veins. With the business functioning so smoothly, I
> decided to delegate the active management to the men with whom I had sur-
> rounded myself who had helped me to do the job in order that I might devote
> my efforts to my new ambitions.[265]

In a July 22, 1930, letter marked "Personal," Tom Huston Peanut Company vice president Walter A. Richards wrote Carver:

I have been planning for weeks to come over to Tuskegee to see you but somehow something always happens at the last minute to prevent my getting away.

As you know, Mr. Huston is busy with his frozen peach plant at Montezuma, which makes it necessary for me to stay pretty close here . . .

I am going to run over as soon as I can and talk over the whole situation with you. [266]

New York City native Clarence Birdseye (1886–1956) is considered the father of the frozen food industry. His first company went bankrupt in 1924, but the same year he persevered and developed a process for packing fresh fish into cartons, then quick-freezing them. He added meat, fruit, and vegetables in 1927. He invented and patented his equipment.[267]

By 1930, Tom Huston was also one of the early entrepreneurs in the business of quick freezing of foods. He established a plant in Montezuma, Georgia, to produce a line called Frosty Morning: Fresh Georgia Peaches.

Tom Huston's Frosty Morning wax cup container in which he would ship and display frozen peaches.

He used the Columbus address of the Tom Huston Peanut Company to link the distribution through his existing sales agents.

To start his quick-freeze business, Huston sought out his banker, the First National Bank in Atlanta. According to Huston, "the Tom Huston Peanut Company was still in excellent financial condition. Of course, sales were off, but earnings were still good, dividends were still being paid to both preferred and common stockholders. And with a well earned surplus to our credit." In normal times, Huston's commitments, which amounted to large sums, could easily have been met. During the Great Depression, business was not so easy. In an autobiographical pamphlet, Huston recalled, "Nevertheless, the obvious thing to do was to try to arrange a large loan to pay my debts and try to clean the slate." However, the bank would not grant the loan without receiving as collateral a controlling stock interest in the Tom Huston Peanut Company. Huston needed the money. Regretfully, he agreed to the bank's demand.[268]

His Frosty Morning idea seems to have been ten years ahead of its time. Grocery stores and other retail outlets did not yet have the equipment needed to keep the products frozen. One year later, that situation, coupled with the effects of the Depression, found Tom unable to afford the loan payment. By 1932, he had lost his beloved peanut business, and the bank took it over. Former Tom Huston Peanut Company vice president Walter Richards was named president to run the company.

Huston, who had never been comfortable in the public eye, and embittered over his loss, became a recluse and eventually moved to Florida, where he started other businesses. In his autobiographical pamphlet, he recalled his dad's old philosophy:

> Son, never cry over spilt milk. Just get busy and drive up another cow. That cow has been driven up and given the name of "Tom Huston System." "She" is now producing Julep Chewing Gum and Sport Pack Peanuts. Good products that deserve your nickels strictly on their merit. FRESHER—because our "system" of distribution gives them to you quicker. A real triumph in modern merchandising, if I do say it myself.

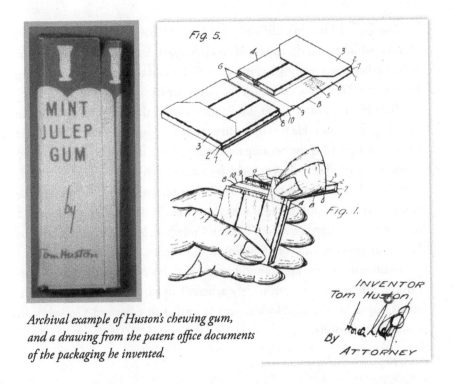

*Archival example of Huston's chewing gum,
and a drawing from the patent office documents
of the packaging he invented.*

Julep Chewing Gum is today's greatest 5¢ value. . . Introduced in 1933, it is
already on sale throughout the entire South and Middle West . . .

Sport Pack Peanuts represent the best "PEANUT" job that I have ever done.
When placed on sale beside older brands, the public readily shows a preference for Sport Pack. [269]

Huston designed and patented a fold-over container that would hold
several sticks of the gum. The gum was not successful, probably because a
near-monopoly on the chewing gum market at that time was held by the
Beech-Nut company. [270]

Using knowledge from establishing his plant in Montezuma, Georgia,
Huston joined with DuPont-Nemours of Jacksonville to establish a chain
of canning factories, beginning in Orlando and Tampa, Florida, to quick-
freeze citrus fruit and citrus fruit juices.

Another of Huston's businesses was the House of Huston in Miami, Florida, which "manufactured pet foods, collars, leashes and medicines, as well as other items relating to pets. In 1958, he sold the company to Sterling Drug Co. of New York, owners of the Bayer Aspirin label for $22 million." [271]

Tom Huston, like Carver, loved flowers and that led him to produce superb quality roses. He was hybridizing a special rose for Florida, a project left unfinished, when he became terminally ill. He developed and patented a peach named "Early Amber" which is still grown in central Florida. Additionally, Huston was interested in abstract photography. He traveled the country and made photographs which are now displayed at universities and museums, including in the Tom Huston Collection located in the Columbus State University Archives in Columbus, Georgia.

Huston shared his talents and fortune with his community. His philanthropic generosity has been widely acknowledged. He died July 20, 1972, at his home in Miami, Florida, and is buried in Linwood Cemetery in Columbus, Georgia.

The Tom's Peanut logo endures today on these peanut storage silos in Columbus, Georgia.

A testament to his legacy is a June 12, 2005, comment on Ancestry.com: "Tom's Foods, with peanut silos that reach 144 feet into the Columbus skyline off 10th Avenue, is one of the largest purchasers of peanuts in the Southeast, and the toasted peanut remains one of the company's best selling products."[272]

GEORGE WASHINGTON CARVER CONTINUED to correspond with Bob Barry and Grady Porter, although not nearly as often as during the team's eventful few years of research and education on the peanut industry. Carver developed a peanut oil formula which he used to provide massages to people with polio, stroke, arthritis, and other muscular problems. The publicity from that effort generated hundreds of letters daily from persons wanting to purchase the oil or receive the massages. Carver worked long hours on the weekends to offer his services to many as possible. He did so up until shortly before his death.

Carver also continued to travel, making talks and presentations all over the country, as his health permitted. He still did not worry about material things: clothes or cars or other signs of being famous. He still received calls from the bank in Tuskegee on a semi-annual basis, reminding him that he had not cashed his paychecks and requesting that he search his desk drawer and find them. The bank would send someone to pick them up and deposit them so the annual bank reports could be completed. Even when he was tired and weak from anemia, he still rose at 4 a.m. and walked the campus as his strength allowed. His need to talk to God and observe the beauty of creation gave him energy to keep going.

Carver was appointed as Collaborator for USDA's Mycology Disease Survey in 1935. To him, it was a supreme honor and brought with it the acknowledgment of his peers at the highest level for the contributions over his lifetime of collecting specimens and donating them to Iowa State University as well as to the USDA. This was recognition he never felt that he received at Tuskegee Institute.[273]

After years of travel back and forth between his Tuskegee laboratory and the Tom Huston Peanut Company, Carver made his last appearance in Columbus in 1939. He was invited by a group of white business leaders to speak at Spencer High School to cool tense race relations and labor unrest

*The George Washington Carver Museum,
on the campus of Tuskegee University.*

at the peanut company, where black males were threatening to strike in support of female workers. He commented later: "I have never heard a finer lot of addresses . . . it shows what can be done when representative people of both races get together. There is absolutely no need for misunderstandings and race riots and all sorts of disagreeable things. Columbus has set the pace for other sections."[274]

Carver, with the suggestions and help of his assistant, Austin Curtis, focused his creativity on developing a museum to house his specimens, research, and paintings. Toward this effort, he donated $30,000 of his life savings. Tuskegee Institute gave him a small building that had been used for the school laundry, located behind Dorothy Hall Guest House [now the Kellogg Conference Center], where Carver lived the last few years of his life. He could walk the short distance from the back of Dorothy Hall to the building. There was also a small greenhouse at the corner of the proposed museum, where Carver's students would bring specimens of his beloved flowers, especially his amaryllis collection, from the larger greenhouse in another section of the campus.

Although the size of the museum was reduced due to lack of funds, Carver was still pleased that he could provide a place for his life's work while he was still living. However, he was not through planning for his legacy.

*The George Washington Carver Research Foundation,
also on the campus of Tuskegee University.*

He wanted to establish a research center where young African American scientists could learn and study without pressure from racial discrimination. The George Washington Carver Research Foundation was built across the street from the Carver Museum; however, this facility was not completed prior to his death in January 1943. Carver left an additional approximately $30,000 to help fund this final dream.

George Washington Carver's Peanut Pudding Recipes

PEANUT PUDDING NO. 1

- - - - - - -

Take one five cent package of Tom's Toasted Peanuts; run through a food chopper using the peanut butter knife.

Grind two teacups of light bread, either stale or toasted. (I prefer the toasted). Grind two moderately large, sour apples; add heaping tablespoon of sugar, and one of butter. Pour in warm water, until it becomes thin enough to pour readily from the spoon.

Cover the bottom of dish with the bread crumbs; spread over this a generous layer of the peanut mixture. Continue this until all is used.

Place in a double boiler and steam until thoroughly done.

Serve with plain butter sauce or real cream.

PEANUT PUDDING No. 2.
(Very fine)

Make exactly as No. 1, except whip an egg, and add another scant tablespoon of sugar. Mix thoroughly and steam as for No. 1.

The above recipies can be varied in a number of attractive ways which will readily suggest themselves to the thrifty and resourceful housewife by adding milk, different fruits, flavoring, extracts, etc., etc.

Afterword

The Legacy of Tom Huston and George Washington Carver's Unlikely Collaboration on Today's Peanut Industry and Research at Tuskegee University

MARCELINE EGNIN, PHD

Professor, College of Agriculture and Environmental Sciences
Tuskegee University, Tuskegee, Alabama

During early periods of innovation and rapid ascent to modern farming practices, as is often manifested in crop and animal domestication and cultivation, humans have manipulated the agriculture sector through technological advancements for improved crop and animal management and production. In the young nation, the offshoot of innovations in United States agriculture to meet food demand cannot be understated. With growing demand for food and protein due to population growth and an increase in American standard of living as the society became more prosperous, the increasing unpredictability of farming, beset by diseases and climatic variability, became a reminder of the need to innovate the sector. To advance crop technology and the agriculture industry, private companies and universities became important allies in the quest of innovation and collaboration. In the early 1900s, one notable partnership for the improvement of the peanut crop and nuts was formed in the southern United States between George Washington Carver, a Tuskegee Institute researcher, and white entrepreneur Tom Huston, a former high school dropout. Both were from rural beginnings but different backgrounds. Yet they were able to create a common ground in collaborative peanut crop improvement innovation.

Peanuts are important food crops grown worldwide today as a multi-billion-dollar industry. Peanut cultivation dates back as far as 300 BC, first by the Incas, then spread to Africa, Europe, and Asia by Portuguese and Spanish explorers upon their arrival in South America around the 1500s. Historical evidence indicates that peanut butter began with the Incas. African were most likely responsible for the transportation and diffusion of peanuts in the United States through the slave trade. Though U.S. commercial peanut farms have existed since the 1700s and 1800s, early utilization of the product remained low, because peanuts were viewed as an inferior food useful mainly for feeding hogs to produce "soft pork" (ref: Regional Food Associated) in the southern U.S. The Civil War marked a turning point for the peanut, as both the Union and Confederacy utilized it as a great energy source, easily packaged and transported.

The development of the American peanut butter types took place in 1895 by William Harvey Kellogg, a physician from Battle Creek, Michigan, who prescribed peanut butter as a source of protein for his older patients with defective teeth. Author Peter Burchard, in a research project for the George Washington Carver National Monument in Diamond, Missouri, wrote that Kellogg obtained the first patent for peanut butter:

> His brother, W. K. Kellogg, was business manager of their sanitarium, the Western Health Reform Institute, but soon opened Sanitas Nut Company which supplied foods like peanut butter to local grocery stores. The Kelloggs' patent for the "Process of Preparing Nut Meal" in 1895 described "a pasty adhesive substance that is for convenience of distinction termed nut butter." However, their peanut butter was not as tasty as peanut butter today, because the peanuts were steamed, instead of roasted, prior to grinding.[275]

The Kelloggs' peanut processing technique differed from that used later by the Tom Huston Peanut Company. The Kellogg brothers would go on to gain fame and fortune by producing cereals. Meanwhile, Carver's critics accused him of claiming to have invented peanut butter, which he never claimed. In any case, by 1904, peanut farming and production gained recognition with the introduction of peanut butter at the Saint Louis World's Fair. More importantly, the U.S. government had instituted agricultural support programs in 1900 aimed at the promotion of important food crops, including peanuts. Additionally, technological advances in nutritious food during World War I and World War II led to a tremendous increase in U.S. peanut farming production.

IN THE EARLY 1900S while the peanut industry was in its developmental stages, Carver was already known as "The Peanut Man" for his work with peanut cropping and disease control. At the same time, Tom Huston, a businessman, was known as the "Peanut King" for his passion for peanut production, snack food, and the development of peanut shelling machines for the Tom Huston Peanut Company. Peanut production in the Gulf States was leveraged by two important contributing factors in the early 1900s: shelling/farm machinery developed by Huston and Carver's Crop Rotation strategy that emphasized peanuts as an alternative crop to cotton. The cotton value chain was severely affected by the boll weevil devastation, leading Extension agents and producers to seek alternative cropping systems; thus began the practice of crop rotation, using peanuts as the prime alternative.

In 1924, when Tom Huston contacted George Washington Carver requesting assistance, the peanut was far from an established crop, since much of the South was still reeling from the effects of the boll weevil. However, by 1927, peanuts were being sold throughout the country and were generating more than $4 million in annual sales. This would not have been possible without the intrinsic partnership of research efforts in understanding peanut development, diseases, and farming.

Huston apprised Carver of his problem with peanut quality and requested his advice on issues he had identified as critical for improving the peanut crop if the industry was to survive. Carver responded with suggestions, and, shortly thereafter, he became an unpaid consultant and technical adviser on peanut research, production, and processing to the Tom Huston Peanut Company. Huston recognized the need to increase the number of peanut farmers, and Carver recommended an increase in outreach and service to farmers. He also predicted that greater recognition of the use of the peanut in the diet would increase the number of households utilizing peanuts, thus boosting demand for the product.

With increased demand, returns from production increased, thus enticing more farmers to engage in peanut production. As peanut growers increased in number, they encountered several peanut diseases which devastated their crops, thus restricting the expansion of the peanut industry. The need for further research to respond to these challenges was answered at the University Experiment Stations. Carver and Huston noted and cataloged every observed incidence occurring throughout the peanut value chain, hoping to find traits critical to peanut breeding that would benefit producers and the industry. Factors such as seed quality and seedling vigor, seed size and weight, as well as the weight and color of shelled nuts linked to variety were investigated. In this effort, Huston's employees assisted Carver in sampling peanut seeds and fungi for identification and strategies to manage the diseases. Carver also documented several diseases, especially that of the leaf: *Cercospora personatua,* which partly or wholly defoliates the plant causing shriveling and wrinkling of the nut; and the disease of the root, *Neocosmospora vasinfecta,* which discolors and shrivels both the nuts and roots, causing field damage of 95 percent of the nuts. From 1927 to 1932, the work of Carver and the team from Tom Huston Peanut Company led to the identification and publication of a list of peanut diseases, especially *Cercospora personatua* and *Neocosmospora vasinfecta.* Their studies gave insight into the inherent instability of the peanut harvest of fresh nuts due to post-harvest fungal diseases. Their observations represent the first and most direct indication of the linkage between fungal pathogens and disease response in plants.

THE TEAM'S OUTREACH AND education plan was designed to inform farmers, producers, and U.S. policy makers about peanut disease-priority research. Carver's early research harnessed the collective vision and broad expertise of the peanut research community. However, his assertions put scientists at odds for historically based distrust reasons. Nonetheless, Carver had the support and trust of Tom Huston. In addition, as the relationship grew and data collection and processing increased, the need for constant communication to handle the quantity of data was evidenced by the hundreds of letters exchanged. While the Tom Huston Peanut Company benefited from George Washington Carver's scientific work, this collaborative work did not receive government support, unlike the Experiment Stations at Land Grant Universities in the Gulf States. Huston did provide resources and support to Carver's work on the peanut disease research and publication, which were used as education outreach. The Huston-Carver partnership played a pivotal role in establishing and expanding the Gulf States peanut industry until 1932. The Tom Huston Peanut Company business was sold during the same year and Tom Huston was no longer involved, although the relationship between Carver and the company continued until Carver's death in 1943.

The impact of the relationship on today's peanut research and industry is readily evident, as peanuts are today the twelfth most valuable cash crop in the U.S. and are grown on some 1.75 million acres with a farm value of more than $1 billion. The crop is a major study topic by university research groups, peanut growers, businesspersons, and farmers. Most importantly, the overall goal—increasing peanut production and consumption—of the Huston-Carver partnership has been achieved. The pioneering scientific and industrial collaboration of Huston and Carver over a commodity fueled the interest of universities, industry, and federal government to begin unique and participatory-collaborative efforts among stakeholders with different backgrounds for the common good and the production of commodities. The impact of the legacy continues in research innovation, public sector infrastructure, commercial development, and delivery systems. The federal government now provides oversight and financial assistance to each state's land grant universities for increasing research and Extension work on peanut production and utilization.

In addition, we now know the nutritional and health value of the peanut. It is considered a low-sodium food, free from cholesterol, and containing less than 20 percent saturated fatty acids—hence, heart-friendly. The seed contains 44–55 percent oil and 22–30 percent protein on a dry basis and is a rich source of minerals (phosphorus, calcium, magnesium, and potassium) and vitamins E, K, and B group. The oil also contains some palmitic, arachidonic, behenic, and other fatty acids. In addition, the peanut has a low glycemic index (a measure of the rate at which carbohydrate breaks down and releases glucose into the blood stream). The amount of protein in peanuts is higher than in eggs, meat, fish, and dairy products.

THE LEGACY OF THE Huston-Carver partnership, as it relates to today's peanut industry and the impact on collaborative agricultural research, is linked to both technical and institutional constraints and opportunities. Worldwide changes have shifted agriculture's focus beyond food and fiber production, to the creation of modern cultivars through collaborative crop improvement and promotion for increasing the utilization of peanuts. New and different roles involve delivering nutritional, pharmaceutical, and bio-based products to provide sound resource stewardship and support of rural communities. In the Era of Agriculture 3.0, which transcends Ag 1.0 and 2.0, with molecular bioinformatics, genomics, biotechnology, and gene editing, these new capabilities are redefining what precision agriculture actually means.

This past collaboration and the future of today's peanut research are intrinsically anchored in research discovery, ingenuity, and imagination to improve crop yield and quality. This is accomplished through seed breeding for higher yields, higher quality, lower levels or no aflatoxin, better flavor and shelf life, more disease resistance, and mitigation of allergenic reaction. Both the government and the industry allocate considerable time and financial resources to peanut research to produce a high-quality food item. The U.S. peanut industry today represents farmers, producers, shellers, manufacturers of allied products, and service companies. The industry strictly enforces government regulation to ensure that U.S. peanuts are consistently of high quality. Additionally, comprehensive lot identification systems enable peanuts to be tracked throughout their various post-harvest stages of storage and handling until final delivery to a domestic processor or exporter.

The continued advancements in peanut/food development have involved contributions by leading academic scientists, coupled with the innovations developed by public and private companies. Research and technology development of modern biotechnology addresses crop and animal production and understanding potential impacts on biodiversity and the environment and promotes strengthening of public institutions and development of policy

frameworks. It also enhances informed decision-making that promotes peanut safety and commercial sector development delivery of new technology
and its integration into market-based, agri-food systems.

The outstanding findings from the Peanut Genome Project funded by
USAID (University of Georgia and a consortium of universities) add a new
level to the continuum of George Washington Carver's research during the
1920s; his collaborative efforts with Tom Huston and are now being conducted in many U.S. universities, including the University of Georgia and
Tuskegee University, Carver's home institution. Traditional plant breeding
has been used since crops were first cultivated. While this method allows
the farmer to improve his crop yield by producing plants that contain the
most desirable traits, such as drought tolerance, climatic resilience, and an
increase in the number of nuts per plant, it also takes a long time, over several
growing seasons, to identify the best traits and produce a more desirable
crop. Make no mistake, today's peanut crop comes from more varieties and
produces higher yields, but too much time is required to choose those plants
exhibiting the best characteristics because of the inability of researchers to
pinpoint exactly which genetic codes contribute to those desirable traits.
The research conducted by the Peanut Genome Project can assist the peanut
industry by: shortening the traditional breeding time, thus reducing production costs; minimizing peanut losses due to diseases; increasing nutritional
value; and addressing safety issues such as peanut allergies.

GEORGE WASHINGTON CARVER'S seminal work is associated with the
expansion of the peanut industry with the research he conducted at Tuskegee
Institute (now Tuskegee University) in Alabama beginning in 1903. The
talented botanist recognized the intrinsic value of the peanut as a cash crop.
Carver proposed that peanuts could be planted as a rotation crop in the
cotton-growing areas of the southeast where the boll weevil threatened the
region's agricultural base. Not only did Carver make a significant contribution to changing the face of southern peanut farming with support from
unlikely stakeholders like Tom Huston, but his research identifying diseases
of the peanut plant proved critical to the survival of the entire peanut crop.
The first of its kind, written specifically for growers, his bulletin entitled

"Peanut Diseases" was published by the Tom Huston Peanut Company and distributed to growers, Extension agents, Experiment Stations, U.S. senators, and USDA scientists. This bulletin raised the issue from the state level to the federal level and created interest that would result in federal funding for the peanut growers and the industry. Carver also identified more than three hundred uses for peanuts, from recipes to industrial products.

At Tuskegee University today, agricultural research serves as the motor for continuing the legacy of Carver and is a driver for crop improvement, aiding not only underserved communities but also creating opportunities to homogenize agricultural systems through collaborative innovation. Using modern bioengineering approaches in research projects funded by the National Aeronautics and Space Agency (NASA), Tuskegee University faculty have successfully developed high-essential-amino-acid peanuts to leverage the methionine deficiency of relevance in meeting protein dietary needs. New technologies, such as CRISPR, to improve peanuts are near-term examples. Tuskegee faculty members are developing novel oil-content and nematode-tolerant traits, relying upon CRISPR-Cas9 genome-editing to create positive impacts in peanuts. In addition, peanut molecular markers, in vitro seed production, and tissue culture regeneration methods are also contributions to the Carver legacy. Moreover, progress in peanut research is evidenced by the positive results of Tuskegee University's recently initiated early development program that introduces soilless production to impact yield index, thus creating a common ground linked to the institutional mandate of peanut research.

Carver's legacy of outreach continues with many K-16 programs at Tuskegee University. For example, through "Disruptive Learning Strategies," minority students are pipelined into new opportunities in precision agricultural biotechnology, especially for the BS and MS degrees in agriculture and food sciences, and more importantly the integrated PhD programs: the Integrated Bioscience (IBS) doctorate and the Integrated Public Policy (IPPD) doctorate.

Appreciation is extended to Dr. Curtis Jolly for critically editing this afterword.

Resources

Agricultural Resource Management Survey (USDA).

American Peanut Council, https://www.peanutsusa.com/about-apc/the-peanut-industry.html

American Peanut Research and Education Society, Tifton, Georgia. See https://apresinc.com

Bertioli, D.J., J. Jenkins, J. Clevenger, et al. The genome sequence of segmental allotetraploid peanut Arachis hypogaea. *Nat Genet* 51, 877–884 (2019).

Burchard, Peter, "George Washington Carver: For His Time and Ours," report prepared for the George Washington Carver National Monument in Diamond, Missouri, National Parks Service, 2005, 100–101.

Dodo, H. W., K. N. Konan, F. C. Chen, M. Egnin, and O M. Viquez, 2007. "Alleviating Peanut Allergy Using Genetic Engineering: The Silencing of the Immunodominant Allergen Ara H 2 Leads to Its Significant Reduction and a Decrease in Peanut Allergenicity. *Plant Biotechnology Journal*, 6: 2135–2145.

Egnin, M., A. Mora, C. S. Prakash, 1998. "Factors Enhancing Agrobacterium tumefaciens-Mediated Gene Transfer in Peanut (Arachis Hypogaea L.). *In Vitro Cellular & Developmental Biology - Plant* 34: 310–318.

Georgia Historical Society

Kramer, Gary R. *George Washington Carver: In His Own Words* (Columbia, Missouri: University of Missouri Press, 1987).

Melancon, J. Merritt Melancon, "First Peanut Genome Sequenced," UGA Today, 2014. https://news.uga.edu/first-peanut-genome-sequenced/

National Agricultural Statistics Service (NASS) of the U.S. Department of Agriculture (USDA). See https://www.nass.usda.gov

Peanut Research Foundation, online site of the Peanut Foundation, Alexandria, Virginia. See https://peanutresearchfoundation.org/.

PeanutBase, "Genetic and genomic data to enable more rapid crop improvement in peanut," is a member of the Legume Federation and is supported by the Peanut Foundation. See https://peanutbase.org/peanut_genome.

Sudhansu Dash, Ethalinda K.S. Cannon, Scott R. Kalberer, Andrew D. Farmer and Steven B. Cannon. "PeanutBase and Other Bioinformatic Resources for Peanut" in *Peanuts Genetics, Processing, and Utilization* edited by H. Thomas Stalker and Richard F. Wilson, 2016 (Urbana, Illinois: AOCS Press, 2016) 241–252.

Tuskegee University Archives. See https://www.tuskegee.edu/libraries/archives.

Tuskegee University College of Agriculture, Environment and Nutrition Sciences. See https://www.tuskegee.edu/programs-courses/colleges-schools/caens

U.S. Department of Agriculture (USDA). See https://www.usda.gov.

Appendix A: Examples of
Tom Huston Peanut Company Documents

Hang This Up

PEANUT GRADES
SMALL WHITE SPANISH FARMERS STOCK
BY U. S. STANDARDS OF THE U. S. DEPARTMENT OF AGRICULTURE

After the SMALL SHRIVELED KERNELS have been sifted through a screen with FIFTEEN SIXTY-FOURTHS of an inch by THREE QUARTERS of an inch slotted holes, the balance of the KERNELS must be as follows:

No. 1 { If there is 70% SOUND & MATURE KERNELS, 2% of DAMAGED & DISCOLORED KERNELS is allowed
" " " 71% or more S. & M. " 3% " " " " " " "

No. 2 { If there is 65% SOUND & MATURE KERNELS, 2% of DAMAGED & DISCOLORED KERNELS is allowe
" " " 66% " " " " " 3% " " " " " " "
" " " 67% " " " " " 4% " " " " " " "
" " " 68% or more S. & M. " 5% " " " " " " "

No. 3 { If there is 60% SOUND & MATURE KERNELS, 2% of DAMAGED & DISCOLORED KERNELS is allowed
" " " 61% " " " " " 3% " " " " " " "
" " " 62% " " " " " 4% " " " " " " "
" " " 63% " " " " " 5% " " " " " " "
" " " 64% or more S. & M. " 6% " " " " " " "

FIGURE OFF-GRADE PEANUTS AS FOLLOWS:

If a NUMBER ONE grade peanut is sold for the figures on the left of each column, then each percent of SOUND and MATURE KERNELS is worth the figure shown opposite, on the right of each column. Multiply the percent of SOUND and MATURE KERNELS in YOUR PEANUTS by the value shown for each percent.

Example:—Peanuts sold at $70.00 Basis No. 1 run 68½% Sound and Mature Kernels and 2% Damaged and Discolored Kernels. Each percent is worth $1.00, so this lot is worth $68.50 per ton.

$65.00 per ton is	$ .93 each %	$77.00 per ton is	$1.10 each %	$89.00 per ton is	$1.27 each %
66.00 " " "	.94 " "	78.00 " " "	1.11 " "	90.00 " " "	1.28 " "
67.00 " " "	.95 " "	79.00 " " "	1.13 " "	91.00 " " "	1.30 " "
68.00 " " "	.97 " "	80.00 " " "	1.14 " "	92.00 " " "	1.32 " "
69.00 " " "	.98 " "	81.00 " " "	1.16 " "	93.00 " " "	1.33 " "
70.00 " " "	1.00 " "	82.00 " " "	1.18 " "	94.00 " " "	1.34 " "
71.00 " " "	1.01 " "	83.00 " " "	1.19 " "	95.00 " " "	1.36 " "
72.00 " " "	1.03 " "	84.00 " " "	1.20 " "	96.00 " " "	1.37 " "
73.00 " " "	1.04 " "	85.00 " " "	1.22 " "	97.00 " " "	1.38 " "
74.00 " " "	1.06 " "	86.00 " " "	1.23 " "	98.00 " " "	1.40 " "
75.00 " " "	1.07 " "	87.00 " " "	1.24 " "	99.00 " " "	1.41 " "
76.00 " " "	1.09 " "	88.00 " " "	1.26 " "	100.00 " " "	1.42 " "

The above takes care of the shortage of SOUND and MATURE KERNELS, if any. If the DAMAGED and DISCOLORED runs over 2%, something must be deducted for each percent over, as it costs about $1.00 per ton to pick out each percent by hand.

SEED PEANUTS

THIS IS THE WAY WE PRODUCE THEM

First the very best SMALL WHITE SPANISH farmers stock that can be bought is set aside for seed.

After being on storage a long time they dry out completely so that there will be no loss in weight, on account of shrinkage, after you get them.

Early in March we clean them up and take out the low grade peanuts in the following way.

They are first lifted twenty feet by air. The air will not lift rocks, nails and other heavy material so such as that is taken out by this operation.

They are then dropped through another draft of air that sucks out the light material such as hulls, stems, etc.

Then they go over a shaking screen. The peanuts go through this screen and the big sticks stay on top of the screen and shake off. This takes out the big sticks, cotton bolls, etc.

The peanuts then go over another shaking screen which lets the small pods and shelled peanuts go through, keeping the largest whole pods on top of the screen.

The large whole pods are then dropped through a draft of air, set so that it will suck out the pops, and most of the peanuts which have a kernel in only one end.

The remaining peanuts are then big, heavy, clean peanuts free from trash and pops. These are put up in 75 pound sacks for seed. We use 75 pound sacks because we think that much should be planted per acre.

When the whole operation is completed only about half of the original peanuts worked are left for seed. These are the best half.

Naturally the farmers stock that has been separated from the seed is the worst half and loses some of its value. This makes the other half, which is the seed, worth more.

We sell, every year, a large tonnage of this seed at cost for cash. If we attempted to sell it on credit we would have to employ an additional office force to keep up with it. Some would fail to pay for it and to take care of that we would have to charge more for the seed.

We put up seed peanuts in the shell because it has proven to be better for this purpose than shelled peanuts. The Creator knew more about peanuts than any man, when He made them, and He is the One that put the shell on it.

The shell will protect the seed from either too much or too little moisture in the ground. The germ in a shelled peanut is apt to be killed by too much heat or rot from too much water in the ground.

Before selling any seed we have a number of germination tests made to see if they will come up alright.

Price quoted on request.

Hope we may have your order.

Tom. Huston, Peanut Co.
Columbus, Georgia
SHELLING DEPARTMENT.

Various Analyses on Commercial Peanut Hulls

Moisture	9.10%	9.83%	7.95%
Fat	2.60	2.37	?
Protein	7.30	10.31	6.85
Crude Fibre	56.60	50.82	60.60
Nitrogen Free Extract	18.90	21.34	17.06
Carbohydrates	75.50	72.16	76.66
Ether Extract	?	?	2.06
Ash	5.50	4.33	5.20

In above, the first set of figures was taken from the book "Feeds and Feeding," by Henry and Morrison. The second set is the average of two samples sent to Law & Co., Chemists, Atlanta, Ga., from the Shelling Plant of the Tom Huston Peanut Co. The third set is the average of 100 samples taken from a Texas Bulletin.

COMPARATIVE ANALYSES
(Taken from the book "Feeds and Feeding" by Henry & Morrison)

	Cotton Seed Hulls	Oat Hulls	Rice Hulls
Moisture	9.70%	6.80%	9.30%
Fat	1.90	1.70	1.10
Protein	4.60	4.00	3.30
Crude Fibre	43.90	29.20	35.40
Nit. Free Extract	37.30	52.30	34.00
Carbohydrates	81.10	81.50	69.40
Ash	2.70	6.00	16.90

MINERAL IN PEANUT HULLS
(Average of 22 samples from a Texas State Bulletin)

Phosphoric Acid	.15%
Potash	1.16
Lime	.31
Magnesia	.25
Insoluble Ash	1.79

SUGAR, STARCH AND PENTOSANS IN PEANUT HULLS
(Average of 35 samples from a Texas State Bulletin)

Reducing Sugar	.588%
Digestible Sugar	1.72
Starch	.737
Pentosans	17.82

PEANUT HULLS — FERTILIZER VALUE
(Sample sent by Tom Huston Peanut Co. to Law & Co., Chemists)

Moisture	9.64%
Avail. Phosphoric Acid	0.70
Insol. Phosphoric Acid	0.04
Total Phosphoric Acid	0.74
Nitrogen	1.23
Equiv. Ammonia	1.49
Potash	1.08

A good many analyses have been published in an effort to show the feed value of PEANUT HULLS.

When peanuts are shelled by hand the hulls show a low feed value. But when shelled by machinery the feed value is greatly increased.

COMMERCIAL PEANUT HULLS are separated from the peanut kernels by machinery, at Shelling Plants. Some of the kernels are mashed, in shelling, and the hulls absorb the oil so released. The hulls are sucked out by air. Many pieces of the kernels are sucked out with the hulls. Some peanut hay also gets in. It is this mixture that is known as COMMERCIAL PEANUT HULLS. The analysis will vary according to the amount of oil, hay and broken kernels in the hulls.

WE GRIND COMMERCIAL PEANUT HULLS TO ANY DEGREE OF FINENESS

TOM HUSTON MILLING CO.
COLUMBUS, GA.

Appendix B: The Plan's Media Blitz

This consisted of press releases to magazines, newspapers, and professional journals, and exhibits at fairs, demonstrations, and presentations. Letters and reports were also mailed to: Agricultural Extension leaders in Washington, D.C., and in the southeastern peanut belt; agricultural researchers at universities and colleges; peanut growers; and others in the peanut industry. The following list is not complete but is representative.

ARTICLES/REPORTS BY BOB BARRY, MGR., SHELLING DEPT.
The Culture and Marketing of Peanuts
Peanut Grades: Small White Spanish Farmers Stock
Report on the Culture of the Virginia Type Peanut in the Southeastern States in 1930
Spanish Peanuts. Jan. 1931
Various Analyses on Commercial Peanut Hulls
Seed Peanuts: This Is the Way We Produce Them, Feb. 1931
List of 75 Different Kinds of Peanuts for Seed, May 1931
More About Peanut Diseases. *The National Nut News* 17–21, Je '31.
Disease Control Experiments With Peanuts. Feb. 1932

ARTICLES/REPORTS BY (OR ATTRIBUTED TO) GEORGE W. CARVER
Bulletin No. 4, 1901: *Some Cercospora of Macon County, Alabama.*
Bulletin No. 31, 1916: How To Grow the Peanut and 105 Ways of Preparing It for
    Human Consumption
"Peanut Milk." *Simmons' Spice Mill,* March, 1920, p. 472.
"Vast Possibilities Offered in the Development of the Peanut Industry." *The Pea-
    nut Promoter.* February 1921, p. 51–53.
"Food Value of Peanut Leads All Vegetables." *The Spice Mill.* March, 1921, p.
    529–30.
"Will the Peanut Industry Survive the Present Crisis?" *The Peanut Journal.* No 15,
    1921, p.13–14.
"Some Possibilities of the Sweet Potato and the Peanut in southern Agriculture."
    For Southern Exposition, March, 29, 1922 (25?)
"What is a Peanut?" *The Peanut Journal* N 7, '23.
"Peanut-Raisin Combination." *The Peanut Journal.* Vol. III, No. 6, Ap '24, p13.
"Possibilities for A New And Promising Industry—-Peanut Flour." *The Peanut
    Journal.* Mar 7 '24. P.5.
"The Possibilities of Peanut Culture in the South," *Manufacturer's Record.* October
    21, 1924.

"The Peanut's Place in Everyday Life." *The Peanut Journal.* 1924, p. 9–10.

"The Peanut Ranks High in Mineral Content." *The Peanut Journal* 13, Ag '25.

"A Great Opportunity for the Farmer" *Manufacturer's Record*, May 21, 1927.

"The Peanut Wonderful" *The Peanut Journal*, August 1927.

"Approves Peanut Week Idea." *The Peanut Journal.* 1927. [In this article, G. Carver discusses two short articles published in previous issue of same journal: the first reflects on the August issue of same journal entitled: Peanut Industry Should Inaugurate National Peanut Week, and the other was entitled: Saving the Waste Products. Also, on same page, no author credited, is a short article entitled: Return of the Peanut that provides a history of the decline and now, the return of the peanut in Charleston.]

"The Peanut Possesses Unbelievable Possibilities in Sickness and Health. *The Peanut Journal* 7: No. 3, 9 Jan. 1928.

"The Peanut and Its Essential Place on the Daily Menu." *The Peanut Journal* 3, Feb. 1929.

"Peanut Diseases and Their Control," *Peanut World* 1 (May 1931):15–17; *Peanut Journal* 8 (May 1929): 9. [Contains an Introduction by Barry and the extensive bibliography by state, compiled by Carver and added to by Barry.]

"Value of all Kinds of Nuts as Nutritive Food. *The Peanut Journal* 11, J1 '29.

"Make Health and Food Value of Peanuts Paramount. *The Peanut Journal* 8: No. 11, S '29.

"Omitting the Big Idea in Peanut Publicity." *The Peanut Journal* 7, S '29.

"Dawning of a New Day for the Peanut." *The Peanut Journal* 25, Ja '30.

"Some Additional Facts On the Food Value of Peanuts" *The Peanut Journal* 13–15, S '30.

"Wasted Food." *National Nut News* 27, Ja '31.

"Some Peanut Diseases and Bibliography/References" February 1931/March 1931 (Published and distributed by the Tom Huston Peanut Company on behalf of G. W. Carver)

"Some Peanut Diseases." Agricultural Research and Experiment Station, Tuskegee Normal and Industrial, Tuskegee, Alabama, February, 1931. 4 p.

"Peanut Diseases and Their Control." *The Peanut World* 15–16, My '31.

"Peanut Butter-A One Hundred Per Cent Food Product." *The Peanut Journal and Nut World* 8, 15, F '31.

"Some Peanut Diseases." Agricultural Research and Experiment Station, Tuskegee Normal and Industrial, Tuskegee, Alabama, February, 1931. 4 p.

"How the Farmer Can Improve the Quantity and Quality of His Peanuts" *The Peanut Journal and Nut World* 9–11, Ap '31.

"Contrary to Former Opinions, Peanuts have Diseases." *The Peanut Journal and Nut World*, 7t, Ap '31

"Huston Peanut Company Studies Peanut Plant Disease." *The Peanut World.* Ap '31.

"How Farmers Can Improve the Quality and Quantity of Peanuts." *The Peanut World* , 9–11, Ap '31.

"How to Prepare Peanuts as a Human Diet." *The Peanut World* 13 My '31.

"How to Prepare Peanuts as a Household Diet." *The Peanut World* 13, Je '31.

"The Best is yet to Come for the Peanut Industry" *The Peanut Journal and Nut World,* 12, Ag '31. [Note at end of article by G. Carver: "Accompanying this bulletin was a circular letter written by Bob Barry in which he credits Carver's incessant work.]

"Are We Starving In The Midst of Plenty? If So Why?" *The Peanut Journal and Nut World,* 13, Ja '32.

"Uses of Peanuts." *National Nut News* Ap '32.

"Peanut and Sweet Potatoes Make for Interracial Peace." *The Tuskegee Messenger* 5–8, Jl '32.

"Dr. Carver Tells Story of Peanut to Students. *The Peanut Journal and Nut World* 18, '32.

"Creative Thought and Action One of the Greatest Needs of the South." *The Peanut Journal,* Nov 1932

"Why Not Change our Method of Advertising." *The Peanut Journal and Nut World* 11, Ag '32.

"The Evolution of the Peanut (Arachis Hypogea): 1st Goober nut, 2nd., Monkey nut, 3rd., the nut of many uses, 4th., Magic or wonder nut." *Peanut Journal,* Nov 12, 1932.

"How Can We Best Fill the Empty Dinner Pail." *Peanut Journal and Nut World,* Feb 1933

"Action Needed Now More Than Anything Else." *Peanut Journal and Nut World,* F '34.

"The Peanut" 1937

"Peanut in Southern Agriculture." *Science Magazine* Date?

ARTICLES/REPORT BY RESEARCHERS, GOVERNMENT OFFICIALS, AND OTHERS

"Advertising Campaign to Increase consumption of Peanuts and Peanut Products." *Simmons Spice Mill,* March, 1920. p.45

Moss, W. W. "Great Creator, Why Did You Make the Peanut?" *The Peanut Journal* 8: No. 3, 47–49, Ja '28.

Hobbs, Ruth. "God, Why Did You Make a Peanut?" *Boys and Girls Comrade* (Anderson, Ind.) 1, Ap 25, '31.

Olsen, George A. "Why Agricultural Gypsum is Essential to Growing Peanuts." *The Peanut World* N 2, My '31.

"Peanut Diseases and Their Control." 16-16, and "Southeastern Fights Peanut Diseases" p.22. *The Peanut World* My '31.

Harden, John W. "Milk Made from Peanuts. *The Atlanta Journal* N 8, p. 7, '31.

"Dr. Carver Tells Story of Peanut to Students." *The Peanut Journal and Nut World* 18, O '32.

"Rusts of Alabama," *The Peanut Disease Reporter* 18: No. 13, 168, N '33.

Miller, Paul R. Peanut Disease Survey in Producing Belts. *The Peanut Journal and Nut World* 14t, D '32.

"Dr. Carver suggests Ways to Stress Food Value of Nuts." *The Peanut Journal and Nut World* 16, Mar '33

"Dr. Carver, Scientist, Shows the Value of Peanuts." *The Peanut Journal and Nut World* 23, S '33.

DePoer, Sarah. Peanut, Second Cash Crop Fast Coming into Rightful Place. *The Peanut Journal and Nut World* 11–13, Mar '34.

[Note: Some references were published prior to the Blitz but are included to show Carver's interest, work, and publications prior to the 1924–1932 time with Tom Huston Peanut Company.]

Appendix C: Introductory Letter to Carver's 'Some Peanut Diseases'

Tom Huston
PEANUT COMPANY

PLEASE ADDRESS REPLY
TO SHELLING DEPARTMENT

Columbus, Georgia   February 16, 1931.

Dear Sir :

For several years we have realized that the farmers are getting less peanuts per acre than they should. Nobody seemed to be sure why, so we determined to find out, for your benefit. In 1930 we not only raised some peanuts ourselves, for study, but also studied many other fields all over the peanut belts of Ga., Ala., Fla., Va. and N. C.

We have learned, without a shadow of a doubt, that most growers are making high yields of peanuts but have been unable to get the TOTAL YIELD in marketable condition. The chief cause of this is DISEASED plants. Many peanuts are left in the ground. Those that are gathered have too much damage. The hay is also damaged.

Don't let this scare you. There is no cause for alarm. It is good news. The fact that this discovery has been made and that DISEASE CONTROL is now being worked out will open the way for MORE PROFIT FROM PEANUTS. You will make as many peanuts, per acre, next year as you ever did. More if there is a dry late season. The diseases have been going on ever since peanuts have been planted. From year to year, as we learn more about DISEASE CONTROL, you will make more peanuts and more profit, per acre.

Dr. Geo. W. Carver of Tuskegee Institute has worked, with us, incessantly on this problem. He is a mycologist of International fame and has become grey in the service. His ability to work out the fine points of peanut problems has been the subject of many books and magazine articles in many Nations. Hence he is an authority of the first magnitude. For years he has proven himself one of the farmers best friends. He has prepared, for you, the attached bulletin. It should help you to help yourself and others to get more for peanuts, per acre, with DISEASE CONTROL. At the first signs of trouble you should have your County Agent investigate. Show him the report also.

We will be glad to supply you with more information next season, but in the meantime please make a study of it too.

Cordially yours,
TOM HUSTON PEANUT COMPANY.

Bob Barry, Mgr., Shelling Dept.

BY THE USE OF COTTON STATIONERY WE ARE HELPING THE SOUTHERN FARMER
WHY DON'T YOU?

The referenced bulletin by Carver is too faded to reproduce, but it can be found in the Tuskegee University Archives.

Notes

1 "A Peanut Romance," *Candy* (Columbus, Georgia: Tom Huston Peanut Company, October 1929), 11. Columbus State University Archives, Columbus State University, Columbus, Georgia.

2 Bradley R. Rice and Harvey H. Jackson, *Georgia: Empire State of the South* (Northridge, California: Windsor Publications, 1988), 158.

3 "A Peanut Romance," 10.

4 "Tom Huston: Fact or Fancy," n.p., (n.d.), 1. Columbus State University Archives, Columbus State University, Columbus, Georgia.

5 Rice and Jackson, *Georgia: Empire State of the South*, 158.

6 "A Peanut Romance," 11.

7 "*A Short History of Columbus, GA 1918–1954*," retrieved July 27, 2019, https:/www.georgiaencyclopedia.org/articles/counties-cities-neighborhoods/Columbus

8 "A Peanut Romance," 11.

9 "Obituary," *Columbus Ledger Inquirer*, (July 21, 1972). Columbus State University Archives, Columbus State University, Columbus, Georgia.

10 "A Peanut Romance," 11.

11 "Tom Huston: Fact or Fancy," 2.

12 Rice and Jackson, *Georgia: Empire State of the South*, 158.

13 "Obituary," *Columbus Ledger Enquirer* (July 21, 1972).

14 "A Peanut Romance," 11.

15 "Tom Huston: Fact or Fancy," 3.

16 *Georgian Sunday* (October 27, 1929). Columbus State University Archives, Columbus State University, Columbus, Georgia.

17 Christina Vella, *George Washington Carver: A Life* (Baton Rouge, Louisiana: LSU Press, 2015), 2–3; Linda O. McMurray, *George Washington Carver: Scientist and Symbol* (New York: Oxford University Press, 1981; Paperback, 1982), 4–6; Gary R. Kremer, *George Washington Carver: A Biography* (Santa Barbara, California: Greenwood, 2011), 6.

18 Mark D. Hersey, *My Work Is That of Conservation* (Athens, Georgia: The University of Georgia Press, 2011), 10–11.

19 McMurray, *George Washington Carver: Scientist and Symbol*, 8–10; Vella, *George Washington Carver: A Life*, 5, 7–8, 340.

20 McMurray, *George Washington Carver: Scientist and Symbol*, 11; Hersey, *My Work Is That of Conservation*, 10–11; Kremer, *George Washington Carver: A Biography*, 5.

21 McMurray, *George Washington Carver: Scientist and Symbol*, 9, 13; Vella, *George Washington Carver: A Life*, 28.

22 McMurray, *George Washington Carver: Scientist and Symbol*, 14; Kremer, *George Washington Carver: A Biography*, 7; Vella, *George Washington Carver: A Life*, 9.

23 McMurrary, *George Washington Carver: Scientist and Symbol*, 16; Kremer, *George Washington Carver: A Biography*, 8; Hersey, *My Work Is That of Conservation*, 12–13.

24 Hersey, *My Work Is That of Conservation*, 13, 17.

25 Kremer, *George Washington Carver: A Biography*, 9.

26 McMurray, *George Washington Carver: Scientist and Symbol*, 19; Vella, *George Washington Carver: A Life*, 19.

27 McMurray, *George Washington Carver: Scientist and Symbol*, 20.

28 Hersey, *My Work Is That of Conservation*, 16.

29 McMurray, *George Washington Carver: Scientist and Symbol*, 23.

30 Hersey, *My Work Is That of Conservation*, 17.

31 Hersey, *My Work Is That of Conservation*, 17–20.

32 Hersey, *My Work Is That of Conservation*, 20–23.

33 McMurray, *George Washington Carver: Scientist and Symbol*, 31.

34 Kremer, *George Washington Carver: A Biography*, 32.

35 Hersey, *My Work Is That of Conservation*,, 29–34.

36 McMurray, *George Washington Carver: Scientist and Symbol*, 41; Vella, *George Washington Carver: A Life*, 44.

37 McMurray, *George Washington Carver: Scientist and Symbol* 35, 39–40.

38 McMurray, *George Washington Carver: Scientist and Symbol*, 34, 37. Also, see: 1904 letter to Principal Washington, 56–57.

39 Kremer, *George Washington Carver: A Biography*, 39.

40 McMurray, *George Washington Carver: Scientist and Symbol* 43; Hersey, *My Work Is That of Conservation*, 46.

41 Hersey, *My Work Is That of Conservation*, 46, 85; Kremer, *George Washington Carver: A Biography*, 46–47.

42 McMurray, *George Washington Carver: Scientist and Symbol*, 87, 295.

43 Osborn to Carver, March 17, 1924. Tuskegee University Archives.

44 Jones to Carver, May 14, 1924. Tuskegee University Archives

45 Rackham Holt, *George Washington Carver: An American Biography* (Garden City, New York: Doubleday Doran, 1943), 226–227.

46 https://en.wikipedia.orr/wiki/peanut. Retrieved 8/11/19.

47 Rob Dixon, "Peanut Production in Alabama," University of Alabama., 1/29/2009, www.encyclopedia of Alabama.org/face/article.jsp?id=h-2016). Retrieved 7/24/17.

48 www.nationalpeanutboard.org/news/these-10000-year-old-peanuts-are-taking-scientists.Retrieved7/24/2017; https://peanutbase.org/organism/arachis/duranesis and htts://peanutbase.org/organism/arachis/ipaensis. Retrieved 8/9/19.

49 https://www.nationalpeanutboard.org/news/these-10000-year-old-peanuts-are-taking-scientists-back-to-future.htm. Retrieved 7/24/2017.

50 http://aboutpeanuts.com/peanut-facts/origin-and-history-of-peanuts/ Retrieved 7/24/17.

51 www.Nationalpeanautboard.ort/peanut-info/history-boiled-peanuts-from -necessity-to-Southern-delicacy. Retrieved 1/2/2021.

52   https://www.feridie's.com/baseball-peanuts. Retrieved 9/11/2019.

53   https://www.app.com/story/life/food/2014/07/29/eat/13324941. Retrieved
     9/11/2019.

54   http://southernpeanutfarmers.org/all-about-peanuts.Retrieved September 18,2018.

55   Kremer, *George Washington Carver: A Biography*, 86.

56   Ron Smith, "Boll Weevil in Alabama," retrieved 11/7/2020, https://www
     .encyclopediaofalabama.org/article/h-1436; McMurray, *George Washington Carver:
     Scientist and Symbol*, 89.

57   McMurray, *George Washington Carver: Scientist and Symbol*, 87.

58   Kremer, *George Washington Carver: A Biography*, 78–79; McMurray, *George Washing-
     ton Carver: Scientist and Symbol*, 114–116.

59   Kremer, *George Washington Carver: A Biography*, 83.

60   Kremer, *George Washington Carver: A Biography*, 107.

61   www.en.wikipedia.org/wiki/depression_of_1920 1921. Retrieved 1/9/2022.; www.
     en.wikipedia.org/wiki/presidency_of_Warren_G._Harding. Retrieved 1/9/2022;
     www.en.wikipedia.org/wiki/McNary-Haugen_Farm_Relief_Bill. Retrieved
     1/9/2022; www.en.wikipedia.org/wiki/Doctrine_of_parity. Retrieved 1/9/2022; www.
     en.wikipedia.org/wiki/History_of_agriculture_in_the_United_States. Retrieved
     1/9/2022; www.u.s.history.com/pages/h3170.html. Retrieved 1/9/2022.

62   https://eh.net/encyclopedia/the-fordney-mccumber-tariff-of-1922/. Retrieved
     1/10/2022.

63   Osborn to Carver, January 31, 1924. Tuskegee University Archives.

64   McMurray, *George Washington Carver: Scientist and Symbol*, 219.

65   *Candy* (October 1, 1929), 11. Columbus State University Archives, Columbus State
     University, Columbus, Georgia.

66   Huston to Carver, October 18, 1924. Tuskegee University Archives.

67   Huston to Carver, October 18, 1924. Tuskegee University Archives.

68   Carver to Huston, October 23, 1924. Tuskegee University Archives.

71   Huston to Carver, October 25, 1924. Tuskegee University Archives.

69   Skip Connett, *Columbus Ledger Enquirer*, Sunday 26, March, 1989. p. E-1.

70   Carver to Tom Huston Peanut Company, April 128, 1926. Tuskegee University
     Archives

71   Huston to Carver, March 5, 1928. Tuskegee University Archives.

72   Carver to Woleban, July 2, 1928. Tuskegee University Archives.

73   Carver to Huston, October 16, 1928. Tuskegee University Archives.

74   Carver to Huston, October 17, 1928. Tuskegee University Archives.

75   Bulletin No. 31, Tuskegee University Archives.

76   Candy, (October 1, 1929), 11. Columbus State University Archives, Columbus State
     University, Columbus, Georgia.

77   Carver to Barry, February 16, 1929. Tuskegee University Archives.

78   Carver to Huston, Sept. 23, 1929. Tuskegee University Archives.

79   Carver to Barry, March 12, 1930. Tuskegee University Archives.

80   Barry to Carver, Aug. 1, 1930. Tuskegee University Archives.

81   Carver to Porter, September 1, 1930. Tuskegee University Archives.

82   Barry to Beattie, August 1, 1930. Tuskegee University Archives.

83   Barry to Carver, August 15, 1930. Tuskegee University Archives.

84   Barry to Carver, August 20, 1930. Tuskegee University Archives.

85   Patterson to Carver, August 30, 1930. Tuskegee University Archives.

86   Carver to Porter, September 1, 1930. Tuskegee University Archives.

87   Night letter to Carver from Barry, September 11, 1930, Tuskegee University Archives.

88   Richards to Carver, September 16, 1930. Tuskegee University Archives.

89   Barry to Carver, September 16, 1930. Tuskege University Archives.

90   Carver to Ross, Sept. 15, 1930. Tuskegee University Archives.

91   Vella, *George Washington Carver: A Life*, 184, 207; Gary R. Kremer, *George Washington Carver: In His Own Words* (Columbia, Missouri: University of Missouri, 1987), 166.

92   Barry to Carver, September 18, 1930. Tuskegee University Archives.

93   Barry to Carver, Sept. 18, 1930. Tuskegee University Archives.

94   Barry to Carver, Sept. 18, 1930. Tuskegee University Archives.

95   Carver to Barry, September 19, 1930. Tuskegee University Archives.

96   Barry to Carver, September 19, 1930. Tuskegee University Archives.

97   Barry to Carver, September 22, 1930. Tuskegee University Archives.

98   Porter to Carver, September 23, 1930. Tuskegee University Archives

99   Memo: Barry to Carver, August 21, 1930, Tuskegee University Archives.

100 Patterson to Carver with encl, Aug. 30, 1930. Tuskegee University Archives.

101 Barry to Carver, December 6, December 10, 1930. Tuskegee University Archives.

102 Barry to Carver, Sept. 18, 1930. Tuskegee University Archives.

103 Barry to Carver, Sept. 23, 1930. Tuskegee University Archives.

104 Barry to Carver, Sept. 24, 1930. Tuskegee University Archives.

105 Barry to Carver, September 24, 1930. Tuskegee University Archives.

106 Porter to Carver, September 25, 1930. Tuskegee University Archives. (Barry to Beattie, Aug. 30, 1930. Tuskegee University Archives.

107 Barry to Carver, September 25, 1930. Tuskegee University Archives.

108 Barry to Carver, September 26, 193/29/1930; 10/16/1930. Tuskegee University Archives.

109 Barry to Carver, October 23, 1930. Tuskegee University Archives.

110 Barry to Carver, September 25, 1930. Tuskegee University Archives.

111 Porter to Carver, September 26, 1930. Tuskegee University Archives.

112 Barry to Carver, Sept. 26, 1930. Tuskegee University Archives.

113 Barry to Carver, September 29, 1930. Tuskegee University Archives.

114 Poole to Barry, Sept. 27, 1930. Tuskegee University Archives.

115 Barry to Carver, Sept. 29, 1930. Tuskegee University Archives.

116 Barry to Carver, September 29, 1930. Tuskegee University Archives.

117 McDowell to Carver, Sept. 29, 1930. Tuskegee University Archives.

118 Barry to Carver, Oct.1, 1930. Tuskegee University Archives.

119 Carver to Barry, October 15, 1930. Tuskegee University Archives.

120 Barry to Carver, October 15, 1930. Tuskegee University Archives.

121 Barry to Carver, October 23, 1930. Tuskegee University Archives.

122 Carver to Barry, October 26, 1930. Tuskegee University Archives.

123 Barry to Carver, Oct. 31, 1930. Tuskegee University Archives.

124 Carver to Osborn, Sept. 11, 1931. Tuskegee University Archives.

125 Barry to Carver, November 29, 1930. Tuskegee University Archives.

126 Barry to Carver, Dec. 10, 1930. Tuskegee University Archives.

127 Barry to Duggar, December 12, 1930. Tuskegee University Archives.

128 Carver to Barry, December 16, 1930. Tuskegee University Archives.

129 Barry to Carver, January 2, 1931. Tuskegee University Archives.

130 Richards to Carver, January 6, 1931.Tuskegee University Archives.

131 Carver to Richards, January 9, 1931.Tuskegee University Archives.

132 Barry to Carver, January 10,1931. Tuskegee University Archives.

133 Attachment: Barry to Carver, January 10,1931, pp. 2–3. Tuskegee University Archives

134 Barry to Carver, January 10, 1931. Tuskegee University Archives.

135 Barry to Cutter, October 15, 1930. Tuskegee University Archives.

136 Barry to Carver, January 12, 1931. Tuskegee University Archives.

137 Porter to Carver, January 12, 1931. Tuskegee University Archives.

138 Barry to Carver, January 14, 1931. Tuskegee University Archives.

139 Barry to Carver, January 22, 1931. Tuskegee University Archives.

140 Carver to Barry, January 19, 1931. Tuskegee University Archives.

141 Carver to Barry, Jan. 19, 1931.Tuskegee University Archives.

142 Barry to Carver, January 20, 1931. Tuskegee University Archives.

143 Porter to Carver, January 21 1931. Tuskegee University Archives.

144 Barry to Carver, January 22, 1931. Tuskegee University Archives.

145 Barry to Carver, January 23, 1931. Tuskegee University Archives.

146 Barry to Carver, February 3, 1931. Tuskegee University Archives.

147 Barry to Carver, February 14, 1931. Tuskegee University Archives.

148 Barry to Carver, February 11, 1931. Tuskegee University Archives.

149 "Tom Huston—Fact or Fancy," undated typescript biography held in the archives of Columbus State University, Columbus, Georgia.

150 William J. Federer, *George Washington Carver: His Life & Faith in His Own Words* (St. Louis, Missouri: Amerisearch, Inc, 2002), 57.

151 Barry to Carver, February 27.1931. Tuskegee University Archives.

152 Barry to Carver, March 9, 1931. Tuskegee University Archives.

153 Higgins to Barry, February 19, 1931. Tuskegee University Archives.

154 Personal communication with Greg Schmidt, Auburn University Archives.12/14/2020.

155 Barry to Higgins, Mar 14, 1931. Tuskegee University Archives.

156 Carver to Barry, March 18, 1931. Tuskegee University Archives.

157 Carver to Barry, March 13 1931. Tuskegee University Archives.

158 Barry to Carver, March 16, 1931. Tuskegee University Archives.

159 Carver to Barry, March 23, 1931. Tuskegee University Archives.

160 Barry to Tabor, March 24, 1931. Tuskegee University Archives.

161 Barry to Carver, March 25 1931. Tuskegee University Archives.

162 Barry to Carver, March 25, 1931. Tuskegee University Archives.

163 Barry to Carver, March 28, 1931. Tuskegee University Archives.

164 Carver to Barry, March 24, 1931. Tuskegee University Archives.

165 Carver to Barry, March 30, 1931. Tuskegee University Archives.

166 Barry to Carver, April 3, 1931. Tuskegee University Archives.

167 Southeastern Peanut Association to Barry, April 4, 1931. Tuskegee University Archives.

168 Barry to Carver, April 6, 1931. Tuskegee University Archives.

169 Carver to George A. Hoadley, 3/1/1929. Tuskegee University Archives.

170 Barry to Carver, April 7, 1931. Tuskegee University Archives.

171 Carver to Barry, April 8, 1931. Tuskegee University Archives.

172 Barry to Carver, April 16, 1931. Tuskegee University Archives.

173 Barry to Carver, April 17, 1931. Tuskegee University Archives.

174 Barry to Carver, May 9, 1931. Tuskegee University Archives.

175 Barry to Carver, May 22, 1931. Tuskegee University Archives.

176 Barry to Carver, May 26, 1931. Tuskegee University Archives.

177 Huston to Carver, May 7, 1931. Tuskegee University Archives.

178 Carver to Tom Huston, May 15, 1931. Tuskegee University Archives.

179 Barry to Carver, June 1, 1931. Tuskegee University Archives.

180 Barry to Carver, May 11, 1931; May 15, 1931. Tuskegee University Archives.

181 Barry to Carver, May 15, 1931. Tuskegee University Archives.

182 Barry To Carver, May 21, 1931. Tuskegee University Archives.

183 Barry to Carver, June 5, 1931. Tuskegee University Archives.

184 Barry to Carver, June 8, 1931. Tuskegee University Archives.

185 Barry to Carver, June 8, 1931. Tuskegee University Archives.

186 Barry to Carver, June 8, 1931. Tuskegee University Archives.

187 Barry to Carver, June 8, 1931. Tuskegee University Archives.

188 Barry to Carver, June 15, 1931. Tuskegee University Archives.

189 *Montgomery Advertiser*, 3-25-2017.

190 Barry to Carver, June 11, 1931. Tuskegee University Archives.

191 Barry to Carver, June 11, 1931. Tuskegee University Archives.

192 Memo: Carver to Barry, 1931. Tuskegee University Archives.

193 Carver to Richards, July 1, 1929. Tuskegee University Archives.

194 Barry to Carver, June 16, 1931. Tuskegee University Archives.

195 Barry to Carver June 26, 1931. Tuskegee University Archives.

196 Barry to Carver July 3, 1931. Tuskegee University Archives.

197 Barry to Carver July 2, 1931. Tuskegee University Archives.

198 Carver to Porter July 6, 1931. Tuskegee University Archives.

199 Ceresan is a disinfectant produced by Bayer Semsan Co., Inc., of Wilmington, Delaware. Its formulation is Ethyl Mercury Chloride 2% and Inert ingredients 98%. The Georgia Experiment Station treated some peanut seed with it and raised the percentage of germination. See Barry to Carver, July 21, 1931, Tuskegee University Archives. Note also, 1. Integrative collaboration is key to scientific and management successes in agricultural production and plant breeding; and 2. Mercury chloride is still in use today as a disinfectant for some in vitro culture work, both as a seed disinfectant and as a surface disinfectant.

200 Barry to Carver, July 8, 1931. Tuskegee University Archives.

201 Barry to Carver, July 15, 1931. Tuskegee University Archives.

202 Barry to Carver, July 20, 1931. Tuskegee University Archives.

203 Barry to Porter, July, 20, 1931. Tuskegee University Archives.

204 Carver to Porter, July 2 1931. Tuskegee University Archives.

205 Barry to Carver, July 24, 1931. Tuskegee University Archives.

206 Barry to Carver July 24, July 30, 1931. Tuskegee University Archives.

207 Barry to Carver, August 5, 1931. Tuskegee University Archives.

208 Carver to Porter, August 5, 1931. Tuskegee University Archives.

209 Barry to Carver, August 7, 1931. Tuskegee University Archives.

210 University of Georgia Archives, Athens, Georgia.

211 Barry to Carver August 4, 1931. Tuskegee University Archives.

212 Barry to Carver, August 8, 1931. Tuskegee University Archives.

213 Carver to Barry, August 10–11, 1931. Tuskegee University Archives.

214 Barry to Carver, August 14, 1931. Tuskegee University Archives.

215 A mattock is a hand tool used for digging, prying, and chopping. Similar to a pickaxe, it has a long handle and a stout head which combines with a vertical axe blade with a horizontal adze (cutter mattock), or a pick and an adze (pick mattock).

216 A mole cricket is a member of the Orthoptera (grasshopper, locusts, and cricket) and is 3–5 cm long in adults, with small, beady eyes and stocky shovel-like front legs highly developed for burrowing. They tunnel through soil and feed on roots and stems of grass. They are present in many parts of the world and may become agricultural pests.

217 Barry to Carver, August 17, 1931. Tuskegee University Archives.

218 Barry to Carver, September 15, 1931. Tuskegee University Archives.

219 Barry to Carver, September 16, 1931. Tuskegee University Archives.

220 Barry to Carver, Sept. 25, 1931. Tuskegee University Archives.

221 Barry to Carver, September 30, 1931. Tuskegee University Archives.

222 Barry to Carver, October 3, 1931. Tuskegee University Archives.

223 Barry to Carver, October 20, 1931. Tuskegee University Archives.

224 Barry to Carver, October 24, 1931. Tuskegee University Archives.

225 Barry to Carver, October 30, 1931. Tuskegee University Archives

226 Barry to Carver, Nov 3, 1931. Tuskegee University Archives.

227 Porter to Carver, October 31, 1931. Tuskegee University Archives.

228 CANDY, Oct. 1, 1929, 11. Courtesy of Columbus State University Archives, Columbus State University, Columbus, Georgia.

229 Barry to Carver, December 15, 1931. Tuskegee University Archives.

230 Barry to Carver, December 23, 1931. Tuskegee University Archives.

231 Barry to Carver, March 10, 1932. Tuskegee University Archives.

232 Disease Control Experiments With Peanuts, February 1932 by Bob Barry and Grady Porter, Tom Huston Peanut Company, Columbus, Georgia. Tuskegee University Archives.

233 Disease Control Experiments With Peanuts, February 1932 by Bob Barry and Grady Porter, Tom Huston Peanut Company, Columbus, Georgia. Tuskegee University Archives.

234 Barry to Carver, April 25, 1932. Tuskegee University Archives.

235 Barry to Carver, April 26, 1932. Tuskegee University Archives.

236 Miller to Carver, May 3, 1932. Tuskegee University Archives.

237 Barry to Carver, June 1, 1932. Tuskegee University Archives.

238 Barry to Carver, June, 4, 1932. Tuskegee University Archives.

239 Barry to Carver, June 2, 1932. Tuskegee University Archives.

240 Barry to Carver, June 16, 1932. Tuskegee University Archives.

241 Barry was referring to a request to Carver that "I have come to realize how much of the peanut I have never yet seen." As noted earlier, he had asked Carver if he would be willing to instruct himself and Porter as to the "microscopic look at cross-sections of the peanut and explain each." Barry to Carver, July 14, 1932. Tuskegee University Archives

242 Barry is referring to a motion made at the convention as follows: "Be it resolved that Mr. Barry be authorized to prepare and transmit to Dr. Carver an appropriate letter of thanks and appreciation, on behalf of this Association for the splendid research work done by him."Linthicum to Carver, July 5, 1932. Tuskegee University Archives.

243 Barry thanked Carver: "I am very glad to learn that you are willing to show us cross sections of the various parts of a peanuts so that we can understand their 'innards' better." Barry to Carver, July 19, 1932. Tuskegee University Archives.

244 Barry to Carver, June 28, 1932. Tuskegee University Archives.

245 Barry to Carver, June 1, 1932. Tuskegee University Archives.

246 Barry to Carver, September 20, 1932. Tuskegee University Archives.

247 Barry to Carver, September 22, 1932. Tuskegee University Archives.

248 Barry to Carver, July 26, 1932. Tuskegee University Archives.

249 [These archives, museum, and papers are no longer available.]

250 Osborn to Carver, June 20, 1932. Tuskegee University Archives.

251 Osborn to Carver, August 9, 1932. Tuskegee University Archives.

252 Carver to Osborn, August 24, 1932. Tuskegee University Archives

253 Barry to Carver, August 23, 1932. Tuskegee University Archives.

254 Barry to Carver, Oct. 21,1932. Tuskegee University Archives.

255 Barry to Carver, letters of August 5 and August 11, 1932. Tuskegee University Archives.

256 Barry to Carver, August 17, 1932. Tuskegee University Archives.

257 Porter to Carver, September 15, 1932. Tuskegee University Archives.

258 Barry to Carver, October 24,1932. Tuskegee University Archives.

259 Barry to Carver, October 26, 1932. Tuskegee University Archives.

260 Huston to Carver, Nov. 15, 1932. Tuskegee University Archives. On personal letterhead.

261 Barry to Carver, December 20, 1932. Tuskegee University Archives.

262 Miller to Carver, February 12, 1934. Tuskegee University Archives.

263 Barry to Carver, May 29, 1934. Tuskegee University Archives.

264 Author Unknown. Columbus State University Archives, Columbus State University, Columbus, Georgia.

265 What Happened To Tom Huston? The Whole Story in a Peanut Shell by Tom Huston. Columbus State University Archives, Columbus State University, Columbus, Georgia.

266 Richards to Carver, July 22, 1932. Tuskegee University Archives.

267 http://en.wikipedia.org/wiki/clarence_Birdseye. Retrieved 10/23/2020.

268 What Happened to Tom Huston? Columbus State University Archives, Columbus State University, Columbus, Georgia.

269 Whatever Happened to Tom Huston? Columbus State University Archives, Columbus State University, Columbus, Georgia.

270 Romanchuk, Rebecca. The Accidental Artefact: Mint Julep Gum by Tom Huston. Out of the Stacks, Archives and Information Services Division Texas State Library and Archives Commission, May 2, 2019. https://www.tsl.texas.gov/outofthestacks/category/artefact-collection . Retrieved 10/23/2020.

271 Tom Huston dies at home in Miami. Columbus Ledger Inquirer, July 21, 1972. Columbus State University Archives, Columbus State University, Columbus, Georgia.

272 www.ancestry.com/boards/thread.aspx?mv=flat&m=. Retrieved 4/15/2020.

273 Kremer. Carver in His Own Word, 83.

274 Amanda Rees, "Tom Huston Peanut Company," April 24, 2017. https://digitalarchives.columbusstate.edu/14-tom-huston-peanut-company. Retrieved 2/21/2021. Columbus State University Archives, Columbus State University, Columbus Georgia.

275 Burchard, Peter, "George Washington Carver: For His Time and Ours," report prepared for the George Washington Carver National Monument in Diamond, Missouri, National Parks Service, 2005, 100–101.

276 Barry to Carver, August 10, 1931. Tuskegee University Archives.

Index

ABOUT THE AUTHOR

EDITH POWELL is a retired professor of immunology and hematology at Tuskegee University. As a native of Tuskegee, Powell has had a lifelong interest in the history of the town and university. Her passion resulted in her role as an independent research consultant on George Washington Carver for the Tuskegee University archives. Powell is also the author of *A Black Oasis: Tuskegee Institute's Fight Against Infantile Paralysis, 1941–1975* (with Dr. John F. Hume) and *To Raise Up the Man Farthest Down: Tuskegee University's Advancements in Human Health, 1881–1987* (with Dana R. Chandler). She is a mother of three with five grandchildren.